D1414920

HOW TO MAKE YOUR OWN
DRINKS
SUSY ATKINS

HOW TO MAKE YOUR OWN
DRINKS
SUSY ATKINS

MITCHELL BEAZLEY

First published in 2011 by Mitchell Beazley,
an imprint of Octopus Publishing Group Ltd,
Endeavour House, 189 Shaftesbury Avenue,
London WC2H 8JY, UK
www.octopusbooks.co.uk
A Hachette UK Company www.hachette.co.uk

Distributed in the United States and Canada
by Octopus Books USA, 237 Park Avenue,
New York, NY 10017 USA

British Library Cataloging-in-Publication Data.
A catalog record for this book is available from
the British Library.

ISBN: 978 1 84533 601 1
Printed and bound in China

MADE BY

Commissioning Editors
Hilary Lumsden
Tracey Smith

Art Direction and Design
Pene Parker

Photography
Noel Murphy

Senior Editor
Sybella Stephens

Text Editor
Hilary Lumsden

Production Manager
Peter Hunt

CONTENTS

Make Your Own
DRINKS

SUSY ATKINS

PHOTOGRAPHY BY
NOEL MURPHY

coffea
Arabica

INTRODUCTION

Do you grow your own fruit and vegetables, or pick wild berries and flowers? Or do you simply have a well-stocked kitchen, refrigerator and freezer? I'll bet that, like me, you care about using natural, fresh ingredients in your cooking. Why, then, do we put up with such awful bought drinks? The usual trip up the supermarket aisle is pretty unappetizing these days (apart from wine), with rows of cheap, bland spirits, sickly commercial liqueurs, and fiercely fizzy, often lurid "soft" options. There are exceptions, of course, but high-quality labels are rare, and they can be enormously expensive.

So let's make our own drinks out of fresh, natural (and often free) ingredients, just as we do when cooking food. I've made a point of using homegrown, foraged, or local cheap ingredients throughout this book to create a wide-ranging selection of tempting drink recipes. And how delicious they've turned out to be: family-friendly cordials from flowers and fruit; fashionable spirit infusions for cocktails and shots; rich liqueurs; hot and cold drinks based on fresh herbs and dried spices. All of these can be made in a short time and are wonderfully tasty. Meanwhile, the transformation wrought by fermenting fruit, vegetables, honey and even weeds and leaves lets you see nature at its most magical.

This is a straight-up, no-nonsense introduction to drink-making at home. Most of your basic ingredients are out in the fields, bushes, backyards and gardens, there for the taking. Let's get started.

The garden and the orchard

It takes a small but significant mind-shift to start making drinks (instead of food) from homegrown produce. Maybe you've never thought of making wine out of your favorite apples, only pies or apple sauce. Blackberries are for jelly and jam, but what about cordials or whiskey? Start viewing produce in a different way—especially anything that regularly produces a surplus.

For drink-making, the most suitable homegrown ingredients include strawberries, raspberries, gooseberries, rhubarb, damsons, apples, pears, plums, blackcurrants, parsnips, red chilies, and various herbs. I've created drinks, both soft and alcoholic, from all these and more after raiding our own vegetable plot and begging quinces, grapes and honey from generous neighbors. In fact, here's a great tip for making drinks from beautiful fresh, local produce: ask around and see what else is ripening in nearby yards and gardens. You might not grow pears or damsons yourself, but there's a good chance that someone who lives nearby does. Be prepared to swap your own harvest or finished drinks to get the staple ingredients you need, but whether it's homemade or bartered, these basic supplies should cost very little.

For city-dwellers, of course, life just isn't like that, yet some ingredients featured in this book are easy to grow in a small backyard or even on a spacious, sunny balcony or patio. These include strawberries, grapes, rhubarb, chilies and herbs. Again, find out which of your friends and neighbors have "patio gardens," or even country homes with an orchard or backyard garden, and maybe offer to help out there in exchange for some precious produce.

Buying from farmers markets and local stores

Large supermarkets stock all the key ingredients needed in this book, both fresh produce and dry goods such as sugar as well as spices and dried herbs. Look for organic fruit and vegetables (always preferable, especially when produce isn't going to be peeled in a recipe), try to pick fruit and vegetables from the country (even better, the region) where you live, and check very carefully for freshness before you buy, smelling and prodding along the way if you can get away with it! Choose unwaxed citrus fruit. Discounts and special offers are great news here, providing a cheap source when you bulk-buy one particular item for a wine or cordial.

Support farmers markets, a hugely useful source of high-quality, locally grown fruit and vegetables, sometimes organic and always in season. Farmers have gluts of seasonal produce, too, so look for cheap and plentiful supplies of all the essential fresh ingredients at particular times of the year and make the most of the harvest. Visiting a farmers market is an especially appealing way to shop, and it's great to support local small businesses.

MAKING SURE YOU USE THE BEST-QUALITY PRODUCE

1 Always use unsprayed fruit and vegetables to avoid getting chemical residues in your finished drinks.

2 Try using natural pest controls such as crushed eggshells, salt or copper rings in your vegetable garden.

3 Use nets to protect any fruit bushes and trees that are regularly raided by birds or wild animals.

4 Pick homegrown produce only when it is truly ripe.

5 Remove any rotten or badly bruised parts of the fruit and wash it all thoroughly to get rid of any soil or natural nasties before using.

Getting ideas and inspiration

So you're busy gathering lots of gorgeous natural ingredients, and you have all the many recipes that follow here to start a brand-new delicious pursuit. It's worth suggesting now, at this early stage, that you keep your eyes peeled for various other sources of drink-making inspiration in order to build up a solid frame of reference. When you're harvesting crops and getting your equipment together, therefore, bear the following in mind.

Make friends with your local home-brewing supplier. There's bound to be an outlet selling home-brewing kits nearby and it pays to get to know the people selling it; they often have years of experience and can offer good advice. I used to turn up at my local store regularly with a bundle of questions. The long-suffering owner passed on a great deal of knowledge, sometimes while selling me little more than a plastic air lock (thanks, Ian, by the way!).

Pester family, friends and neighbors for their own ideas. Wine, cider, mead, and spirit infusions in particular are ancient traditions, and they have evolved in different regions and countries with slight (or more radical) variations, mostly to use specific, locally grown fruit and vegetables. Often it's the people living around you who provide inspiration, so ask around at work or at any clubs you belong to and see if anyone else is "making their own." Putting an ad in your local or regional newspaper or magazine is another way to find fellow drink-makers, or check out associations online. Family members may also have old recipes hidden away and should be delighted to pass them on.

Search for old books in secondhand bookshops and libraries. Although little has been written on drink-making lately, the 1960s–80s proved to be a "golden age" for this subject. Plenty of dog-eared, wine-stained books from this era are still around (although some of the old photography is spectacularly bad!).

Use the internet for tips on drink-making by all means, but tread carefully. There are some useful websites out there, but there are some pretty useless ones, too, and a few that are just plain bizarre. Be selective.

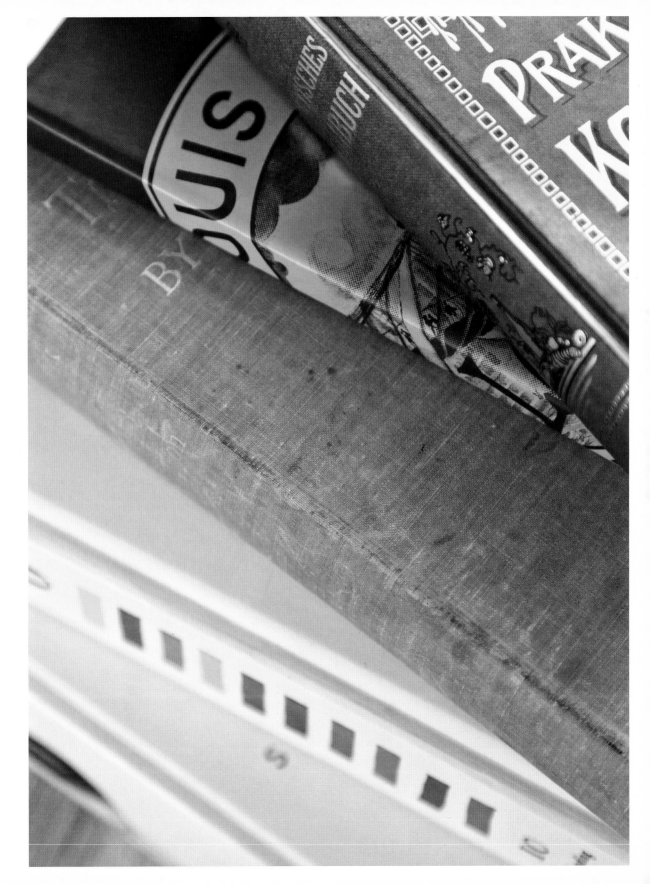

Preserved fruit and vegetables

Out of season, the pickings can look a little lean. Do you really want to make wine out of slightly sad, underripe fruit that has been flown halfway across the world? You might as well buy cheap Chardonnay from the same place. At the farmers market in winter the main crops may be turnips or red cabbage, and I'm not going to suggest you start fermenting those! So "out of season" is when you might want to consider using frozen or canned fruit and vegetables (yes, really!) to make wine.

With a few provisos, go for it. Frozen fruit is particularly good. I've made plenty of drinks out of frozen currants, elderberries, blackberries, damsons and gooseberries in particular and the quality has been fine. Frozen strawberries and raspberries are somewhat less successful for making wine, but they will create reasonable soft drinks and infusions. Sloes, also known as sloe berries, are even better after a quick freeze (see page 76). Parsnips can certainly be used after freezing (freeze as raw chunks, see page 105). Canned and bottled fruit can be considered—a decent cherry brandy or cherryade can be made from canned cherries, for example (see page 140)—but in general, fresh is definitely superior.

Wine made out of dried fruit, including apricots, raisins and even figs, is possible, but consult a specialist book for this. I prefer the flavors of fresh rather than dried fruit in my drinks, and this book contains only one wine with dried fruit in it: Rice and Raisin Wine (see page 108). That said, there's nothing to stop you from experimenting.

Foraging for ingredients

There's a case to be made for saying that foraging for your own is even better than growing your own! Let nature do the hard work, and when the wild fruit or leaves are at their best, get out on a sunny day and grab them from nature. I say "sunny" deliberately. Wild crops tend to taste better if picked on a bright, dry day rather than when it's dark and damp; flowers in particular will have a much better aroma.

Make sure you dress for the occasion. We're talking long-sleeved T-shirts, long pants, sturdy shoes or boots, gloves and even a hat. Sounds excessive? Not really. It's a strange thing, but most of the wild ingredients featured in these pages seem to grow in the middle of thorns, or surrounded by stinging nettles, or else they're high up a tall tree, or on a steep slope or buried in a thicket. Unless you're a giant, you'll be pulling down high branches to get to certain crops, bringing down leaves, twigs and insects on your head in the process. So be prepared and cover up! Oh, and make sure you have insect repellent, calamine lotion and anti-inflammatory medicine at the ready for those inevitable bites and stings.

Take plenty of plastic bags and containers with you for bringing your crops home, and if driving a long way on a hot day consider packing an ice chest or cooler to keep any fruit or leaves fresh. One or two "don'ts:" don't pick beside a busy road (as much for the dust and exhaust fumes on the crop as for the danger), or where chemical sprays have been used (e.g. right next to manicured public gardens). Don't pick where many dogs are regularly walked (extra aromas aren't required, thanks), or where grumpy bulls reside. And never trespass.

This is just sensible stuff, and all that said, it's a joy to go out into the wild on a beautiful day foraging for ingredients with which to make drinks. Dandelions, blackberries, elderflowers and elderberries, rosehips, nettles and oak leaves are out there for the taking, and they all feature in recipes in this book. Take a picnic, your children, a good book and make a day of it!

TIMING AND SEASONS

I strongly advise making drinks from ingredients that are in season. They'll taste fresher, "truer" and better all round if they've been grown according to their natural ripening season, with minimal intervention, and sourced relatively locally—even if you're buying in the crops from a large store rather than growing your own.

As for homegrown, seasonality is everything of course, and you'll want to swoop down on key ingredients at exactly the right moment: i.e. when ripe and ready, but before they turn that overripe corner. It really pays to keep in touch with the neighbors here, swapping your excess fruit and vegetables. If you're not a gardener, keep an eye on nearby farmers markets so you can get exactly the right natural ingredients quickly when the time is right, all tasting their very best.

Spring and summer cropping

The moment in spring for starting to make drinks from homegrown or wild ingredients is when some of the flowers you might use have started to hit full bloom. Tradition in my home country of England dictates that you pick them on April 23, St. George's Day, but in the US, their season is usually much earlier (almost year round in some places), and will vary depending on where you live. So make Dandelion Wine (see page 46) whenever you see them blooming. After that, the first elderflowers should be ready (see pages 42–45).

Rhubarb is the first fresh ingredient I ferment each year (see page 60), followed by strawberries and gooseberries (see pages 56–7), although leave the latter to get ripe and pink if you want a rosé wine from it. Oak Leaf Wine can be made from the first young green leaves, or wait until high summer for a more full-bodied, tannic white (see page 75).

Not surprisingly, midsummer is a season of great opportunities for a drink-maker. Roses and lavender bushes bloom, and the green herbs' heyday is followed by blackcurrants and redcurrants (although these are still rare in most of the US), raspberries, and more strawberries. Late summer sees the start of the apple and plum season and, in a hot year, blackberries are already starting to turn purple.

At the height of summer—July and August—many of us disappear for a week or two on vacation, sometimes leaving our most tempting fruit to the mercy of birds and wild animals, or, sadly, to turn ripe or rotten even before they've been picked.

SPRING AND SUMMER CROPS

SPRING	SUMMER		
Elderflowers	Blackberries	Mint	Rose petals
Dandelions	Blackcurrants	Nettles	Sage
Green gooseberries	Chamomile	Oak leaves	Strawberries
Mint	Cherries	Pink gooseberries	Thyme
Nettles	Chilies	Plums	
Oak leaves	Cucumbers	Raspberries	
Rhubarb	Damsons	Redcurrants	
Rose petals	Lavender	Rhubarb	

Fall and winter cropping

Fall is a glorious time for drink-making. It's apple-picking season, of course, and many species of pears are ripe, too. Both crops have a long ripening period, so there should be no huge rush to harvest and press. To check if an apple or pear is ready, pick one from and cut into it; if the outside layer of the seeds is still creamy-white, then the fruit is underripe. Brown seeds mean a riper crop. You can have several picking, pressing and drink-making sessions throughout the autumn if you have an abundant orchard harvest (see pages 92–101).

Blackberries can have a long season, too, starting to ripen in the late summer but going strong through the fall, depending on how much sun is shining on each bush. Again, expect to do several picking sessions over several weeks, though stop picking when the berries grow squishy and cobwebs drape the bushes (see recipes on pages 66–9). Elderberries, grapes, damsons and quinces are all earlier autumn crops, while sloes (the fruit of blackthorn bushes, often called "sloe berries") and rosehips will be ready in late fall, long after the first frosts (sloes are improved by a natural freeze; see recipes on pages 76–7).

Winter doesn't bring much from nature's stores, although you can pull up the last parsnips for wine. This is the season for making drinks from kitchen basics and other ingredients, such as honey, eggs and spices (see pages 122–31).

FALL AND WINTER CROPS

FALL			WINTER
	Damsons	Quinces	
Apples	Elderberries	Raspberries	Parsnips
Blackberries	Grapes	Rosehips	Rosehips
Chilies	Pears	Sloes	

THE TEN ESSENTIALS

1. STERILIZING AND CLEANING EQUIPMENT

Buy powder or tablets (such as Campden tablets) for sterilizing drink-making equipment from home-brewing suppliers. Use in solution to sterilize all your equipment, including all containers, air locks, bungs, siphons, spoons, mashers and jugs, and always rinse well afterwards with plenty of cold water. Be sure you have a long-handled bottle brush, dishwashing liquid and plenty of new sponges and dish towels for cleaning and drying.

2. PANS AND BUCKETS

A large metal preserving pan (preferably two) is essential for mashing, macerating (soaking), and cooking fruit or vegetables. Some people use a simple food-grade plastic bucket on the floor for mashing or soaking, but I use large stainless-steel pans at kitchen-counter level.

3. MEASURING CUPS AND JUGS

One large and one small food-grade plastic or glass jug and cup with clear measurements on the side are crucial for drink-making.

4. FUNNELS

You will need large and small funnels, including at least one with a narrow end small enough to fit into the neck of an ordinary wine or beer bottle. These can be used for adding powder as well as liquid ingredients.

5. SCALES

You can use approximate measures like teaspoons or cups, which I've listed in this book, but scales are really more accurate, capable of weighing small amounts of powdered ingredients such as yeast or citric acid. Electronic scales are recommended.

6. MUSLIN BAGS AND SIEVES/STRAINERS

You will need muslin or fine cheesecloth and/or fine sieves or strainers to strain your drinks. Muslin is best for wines, but fine sieves are better for tisanes or getting the seeds out of cordials (you can even use a tea-strainer for a small quantity). I prefer clean, new muslin bags, which are inexpensive and can go straight on the compost pile afterwards, together with the discarded fruit! You can also make your own from muslin remnants.

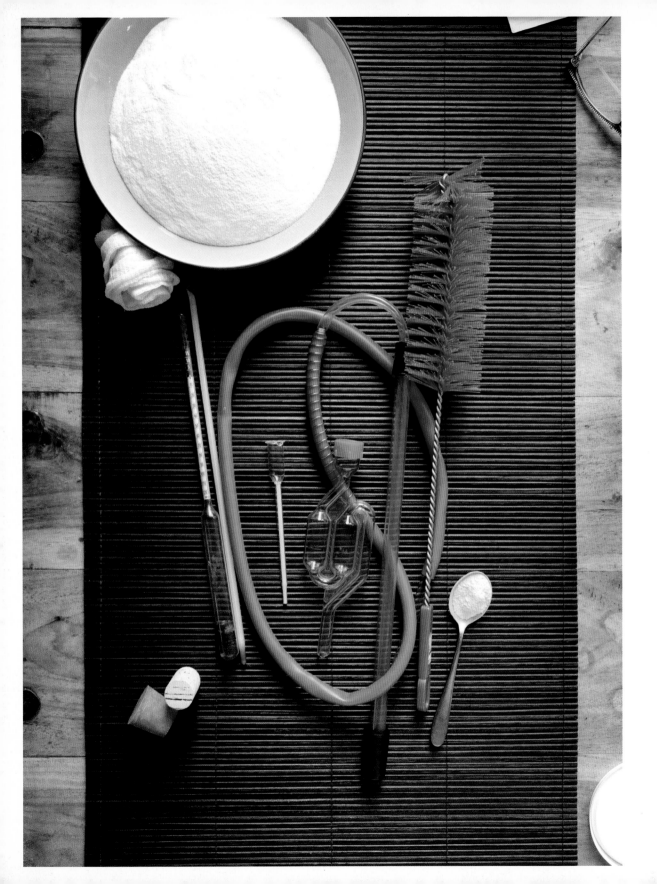

7. SIPHON

This is a long plastic tube that is used to move liquid from one container to another; it's great for "racking off" wine, mead or beer (taking the liquid off the yeast sediment; see page 30) and when bottling. Use it by putting one empty container or bottle at a lower height than the full one, put one end of the siphon into the bottom of the liquid, and suck gently until gravity does the rest for you. Warning! This takes a little practice, and you need to have all the containers that are to be filled ready so that you don't have to stop and start the process.

8. DEMIJOHNS

The most common demijohn is a one-gallon glass jar with a narrow top that holds a bung and air lock (aka fermentation lock), and is the most common vessel used for fermentation by amateur brewers. You can buy cheaper plastic versions, but they're not nearly so attractive.

9. AIR LOCKS AND BUNGS

To keep bad bacteria out of the demijohn, fit a sterilized rubber bung with a hole in it that holds the air lock. The bung is usually rubber; the air lock can be glass or plastic (I prefer plastic because glass air locks break easily). Pour a little sterilized or distilled water into the air lock. The carbon dioxide bubbles up from your fermenting drink and escapes, yet no air can pass back into the demijohn. Fit both components tightly.

10. THERMOMETER

Yeast won't work if it's added to a liquid that's too hot; in fact, it will die. Make sure your base drink is under 86°F to be on the safe side, using a long kitchen or candy thermometer to check (you can buy special brewing thermometers, but these aren't essential). Be aware that it can take a hot liquid in a sunny kitchen hours to cool to under 86°F. Try to be patient; I learned this one the hard way. Still, you can always add more yeast down the line if you've frazzled the first batch!

OTHER EQUIPMENT

Make sure you have some everyday kitchen equipment on hand: teaspoons; tablespoons; a good, solid potato masher for crushing fruit; sharp knives; a large grater (for ginger) and a small nutmeg grater (for spices); and a pestle and mortar. A simple citrus-fruit squeezer may be handy if you don't have the hands of a playground bully.

They're not crucial at first, but the enthusiastic drink-maker might want to invest in other items, especially a hydrometer, which is used to estimate a liquid's alcohol level by measuring the density of the fluid. This is a little like a wide, heavy thermometer with levels written on the side. It is suspended in the fluid both before and after fermentation, and the last reading subtracted from the first gives you an approximate idea of the alcohol level. Another handy gadget is a hand corking machine, which slots new corks into wine or beer bottles.

Extra ingredients

Sugar

The recipes in this book mainly use white sugar, but occasionally I've suggested using brown sugar in the tips that follow, for extra richness. Use ordinary, inexpensive granulated sugar whenever a liquid is hot or to be heated; it will dissolve easily. Use superfine sugar and, best of all, brewer's fine powdered sugar when adding to cool fluid. The latter can be found in home-brewing suppliers and on the internet.

Yeast

Buy small amounts of yeast regularly from a home-brewing supplier to make wine, hard cider, and mead. I find that wine yeast, sold in a pack with nutrient added, is suitable for most purposes; the nutrient feeds the yeast and helps it along. Follow the instructions on your particular brand of yeast, but remember that you might need only a proportion of a large pack for just one demijohn. Buy brewer's yeast for beer and baker's yeast for ginger beer. You can find out much more about the various yeast strains and the effect they have on fermenting drinks by reading specialist books and articles. Throw out old yeast, especially opened packs—it's inexpensive stuff.

Citric acid and citrus fruit

Certain drinks need an extra refreshing tang added to balance flavors in the form of citric acid (in powder form) or lemon juice and lemon rind. Buy fresh citric acid sachets from a home-brewing or winemaking supplier, and stock up on fresh, ripe, unwaxed and preferably organic lemons. Citric acid is also a natural preservative.

Pectic enzyme

A few drinks benefit from a pinch of pectic enzyme powder added to destroy pectin and any resulting cloudiness in the liquid. This is available from home-brewing suppliers; I've indicated when to use it in one or two recipes.

Base spirits

Always buy good-quality base spirits. I don't mean premium vodka or gin, but just relatively inexpensive brands from a reliable store. See page 122 for more advice.

MAKING, STORING AND AGING

Some drinks in this book, such as teas and cordials, are easy to make, but it helps to get the lowdown on those that involve fermentation.

Fermenting and infusing

Keep any drinks that are fermenting or infusing in a cool, dark place: not too cold in the case of fermentation, or the process will slow down to a frustrating snail's pace. You can see how fast your drink is fermenting by watching the bubbles in the air lock. Expect at least four bubbles a minute, even more when the yeast is working at its hardest.

Demijohns can sit in any coolish, shady corner inside a house, but be sure to keep them out of the sun. In winter, fermentation tends to be quieter, so to speed things up, simply move the fermenting drink to a warmer room. And if you're worried about losing the color of a prettily hued wine or other liquid (especially pink drinks), consider making it in a brown-glass demijohn. This should prevent the color from fading as fast.

Racking off

It's important to rack off a fermenting drink properly in order to remove the dead yeast sediment (or "lees"). The siphon method is explained on page 27. Where a wine or beer has produced or "thrown" a lot of sediment, you might need to go through this process more than once before bottling. You can buy stabilizing powders from home-brewing suppliers if you want to stop fermentation earlier than nature would in order to create a crisp, neutral style, and fining (clarifying) powders can be added to help settle fine particles in a very cloudy liquid. I prefer to keep intervention to a minimum, however.

To age or not to age your wine

Don't be afraid to keep/age your wine in demijohns after fermentation has finished, before or after racking off. It can mature there very well, and instead of early bottling, I've found this useful in the case of wines such as Oak Leaf Wine and Parsnip Wine (see pages 75 and 105). Conversely, if you want a youthful, bright, crisp style of wine, make sure it ferments relatively quickly in a warm room, consider stabilizing it after a few weeks to stop further fermentation, then bottle and drink it quickly.

How to keep drinks

Once your drinks are bottled, keep wine and spirits as you would bought ones: in a cool, dark place, resting on their sides if a cork is used, or in the refrigerator or freezer in the case of cordials. Once opened, light wines will last at least three days if resealed and stored in a cool spot, while opened cordials, liqueurs, and spirit infusions should keep for several weeks.

TROUBLESHOOTING

The recipes in this book are refreshingly easy to make, but there can be problems with drinks that involve fermentation. Here are some of the most common conundrums—and how to solve them.

Problem	Solution
Fermentation doesn't start at all.	You may have killed the yeast by putting it in liquid that was too hot, or maybe you used old yeast. Make sure you have fresh yeast and simply add the same quantity to the liquid again, removing the bung for a very short time only.
Fermentation starts but stops far too early.	This often happens in winter when jars are stored in a cold room. Move the fermentation vessel to a warmer place.
Fermentation is fast and furious, leading to liquid bubbling back through the air lock and spilling down the sides.	This isn't a disaster, and should last only a short time. However, you'll need to clean the air lock and bung and replace them regularly while it's happening. Or consider using a cotton stopper for a few days during the first vigorous fermentation, replacing it with the air lock and bung after things settle down.
The water in the air lock turns black.	Take the air lock out, covering the hole in the bung with a napkin or paper towel. Empty, wash and sterilize the air lock thoroughly, fill it with fresh water and replace it as quickly as possible. The "bad" water should not have gone into your fermenting liquid so don't worry. (You may want to use water with a little sterilizing powder dissolved in it if this happens a lot.)
The finished drink tastes synthetic and slightly chemical.	You may not have rinsed all the sterilizing solution off your bottles or stoppers before using them. Always be careful to rinse anything that has been sterilized. Another cause might be overuse of stabilizer (see page 30), which some people think gives a slightly "concrete" taste to wine. Consider dropping this practice; instead, wait until a wine stops fermenting naturally.
After bottling, the wine tastes and smells musty, like damp cardboard.	I'll bet you're using natural cork stoppers! The wine is "corked;" in other words, it has been affected by a taint created by the cork bark. Be sure to sterilize and rinse corks thoroughly before use, or switch to screw-caps or flip-top bottles instead. (I don't use synthetic corks; they're tricky to get in and out of bottles.)

BOTTLES

You can use brown or green bottles, but I prefer clear ones so that I can see the attractive glints of light and color in a finished drink. Of course, it's entirely up to you whether to use old glass wine bottles with screw-caps or corks, beer or ginger ale-type bottles, or plastic containers for bottling your drinks. But there are a few things to keep in mind:

1. Make sure the container and lid are squeaky clean and sterilized.

2. Never transfer liquid that is still fermenting into closed containers unless you're absolutely sure they're strong enough to withstand the pressure of any carbon dioxide that's given off.

3. Fermenting liquids with tightly closed lids can cause plastic and glass bottles to explode. Loosen and re-close the tops from time to time, turning your face away as you do so to avoid possible injury.

A NOTE ON FILLING

Be careful when filling any demijohns at the start of the fermentation process. The liquid should reach to just under the neck, but it may need topping up with cold, boiled water because of evaporation during the boiling, reducing or macerating processes. Conversely, leave some space in containers of homemade drinks that are to be frozen because the liquid will expand a little as it freezes.

GIVING DRINKS AS GIFTS

It's oh-so-easy to grab a bottle from a store to give as a birthday present or take to a party, but how much more impressive to bring along a drink you actually made yourself! Homemade drinks are up there with homemade truffles or jams, in my view. Actually, they are a lot more fun than jam, come to think of it!

It's a good idea to put your drinks into attractive bottles and jars, though, so save any stylish glass containers that come your way, washing and sterilizing them thoroughly before pouring your precious concoctions into them with a funnel. Particular styles of wine come in unusual, appealing bottles—for example, certain sweet French Muscats or Provençal rosés—so keep an eye out for "empties." Mason or ball jars for drinks are also nice to give away, especially in the case of spirits and liqueurs.

If the drink has ingredients in it such as lemon peel, cinnamon, blackberries or lavender, take a long, hard look at it and see if these need taking out, or just replace them with a small fresh piece or a few new berries purely for visual appeal. In short, ask yourself: does it actually look attractive? If not and the drink has finished fermenting, strain out the pieces and decant the liquid into a fresh bottle.

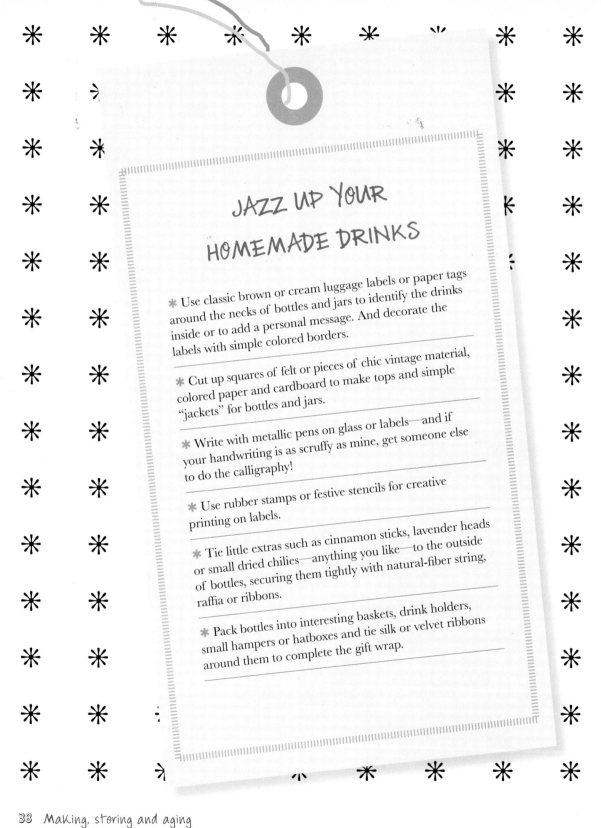

JAZZ UP YOUR HOMEMADE DRINKS

✳ Use classic brown or cream luggage labels or paper tags around the necks of bottles and jars to identify the drinks inside or to add a personal message. And decorate the labels with simple colored borders.

✳ Cut up squares of felt or pieces of chic vintage material, colored paper and cardboard to make tops and simple "jackets" for bottles and jars.

✳ Write with metallic pens on glass or labels—and if your handwriting is as scruffy as mine, get someone else to do the calligraphy!

✳ Use rubber stamps or festive stencils for creative printing on labels.

✳ Tie little extras such as cinnamon sticks, lavender heads or small dried chilies—anything you like—to the outside of bottles, securing them tightly with natural-fiber string, raffia or ribbons.

✳ Pack bottles into interesting baskets, drink holders, small hampers or hatboxes and tie silk or velvet ribbons around them to complete the gift wrap.

FLORAL DRINKS

Making drinks out of flowers sounds like something a child would do; pounding up Grandma's dahlias to make her a cup of tea seems reasonable when you're four. Yet it is possible to make some genuinely tempting drinks from certain blooms, both wild and cultivated. Admittedly, the repertoire is somewhat limited. Only a few flowers can be used, but thankfully, those available are fairly common. Who doesn't have access to roses, lavender, or (far too many) dandelions?

Several of your senses will revel in these drinks. Not only are they visually stimulating and attractive while gathering, making, and on completion, but each has a beguiling perfume. Oh, and they taste good, too. Pick flowers on sunny, dry days; choose healthy, clean heads in full bloom and avoid any browning petals. Finally, only pick flowers close to the time you will use them since they don't keep well.

Elderflower Cordial

*Makes just
over 2 quarts*

*Keeps for 1 month
in the refrigerator*

Frothy, white elderflower blossoms and their sappy, sweet scent beautifully conjure up thoughts of sunshine. I used to make this cordial in small quantities and drink it for only a few weeks each year; now I freeze plenty to ensure that it's available year round. I've tried a few versions, but this is my favorite. Once it's made, pour a measure over ice, then dilute with water to taste for delicate, refreshing drink.

4 lb (about 9 cups) sugar
2 quarts very hot water
25 elderflower heads
1 tbsp citric acid (see page 29)
3 limes
1 lemon

1. Put the sugar into a preserving pan and add the hot water, stirring until the sugar has dissolved. Cool for 20 minutes.
2. Meantime, shake the flower heads over the sink to remove any dust or insects, then swish them gently in a bowl of cool water. Strain and shake until semi-dry.
3. Using small, sharp scissors, carefully snip off all the main stalks and as many of the medium-sized ones as you have time to do, leaving only the floral sprigs.
4. Push the flowers down into the warm sugar syrup and add the citric acid. Stir.
5. Pare one-third of the thin outer rind from the fruit and add to the pan, then slice the semi-peeled fruit and add it, too.
6. Stir everything well, cover tightly, and keep in a cool, dark place for 24 hours.
7. Strain through muslin into a clean pan, then bottle.

* *Freezes well in small plastic drink bottles. Don't fill completely when freezing, and leave some room for the frozen liquid to expand.*

* *Be careful when opening older bottles of cordial: they may have started to ferment. To avoid this, keep them very cold, drink them quickly, or freeze them until needed.*

* *Dilute the cordial with carbonated as well as still water.*

* *I think the perfumed nature of the limes works well here, but you can make this using just lemons. Use fewer of them, though, since they tend to be larger and sharper.*

* *Add peeled, thickly grated root ginger at the same stage as you dissolve the sugar to add a subtle peppery, earthy note.*

* *Combine the cordial with chilled dry (brut) sparkling wine for a simple but wonderful aperitif. Cava works particularly well here because it's fairly neutral.*

* *Make elderflower cocktails by mixing the cordial with gin or vodka plus a splash of lemon or lime juice. I always add a sprig of lightly bruised fresh mint.*

Elderflower "Champagne"

Makes 1 gallon

*Best enjoyed fresh,
but will keep for
several weeks stored
in a cool, dark place*

A mildly alcoholic, softly spritzy wine that's a cinch to make (but see the warning below!). Elderflowers should have enough natural yeast on them to create the fizz without any additions, although you can add a pinch of dried yeast if fermentation doesn't start spontaneously.

This is a similar process to making cordial, but here the liquid is allowed to ferment. For that to happen you mustn't kill the natural yeast on the flowers by plunging them into hot sugar syrup, hence using cold water here.

Warning: the fizz in this "Champagne" is highly unpredictable and varies from batch to batch. Be sure to use strong bottles, preferably thick glass ones with flip-tops, and open them with caution. Check any stored bottles regularly and release gas as a precaution from time to time, especially if you've used extra yeast.

25 elderflower headss
2 lemons
1 lb (2¼ cups) superfine sugar
1½ tbsp white-wine vinegar
1 gallon cold water
pinch of dried yeast (optional, see above)

1. Shake the elderflower heads well to remove any insects, then cut off the main stalks. Don't wash them. Put them in a very clean bucket, add the thin outer rind of the lemons, then their juice.
2. Add the sugar, vinegar and cold water and stir until the sugar has dissolved.
3. Cover tightly with muslin or a dishcloth and leave to stand for several days; check every day to see if fermentation has started. If it hasn't after 3 days or so, add a pinch of dried yeast, stir, and wait a little longer. Bottle.

* *This drink is slightly cloudy, and will throw a sediment with time. This is harmless, but you might want to discard any from the bottom of the bottle.*
* *Lemons work better than limes in this recipe. Increase the amount of fruit used for a sharper tang if desired.*
* *Serve this with a light lunch of undressed leafy salad, mild goat cheese and fresh tomatoes.*

Elderflower Wine

*Makes 1 gallon
plus 3 cups*

*Will keep for
1–2 years*

I confess that I've only made this once or twice because I adore the Cordial and "Champagne" so much, and I like to leave some blooms to turn into berries for Elderberry Wine (see page 70). However, some people absolutely love this, and it has an appealing, light, Muscatty taste.

**approximately 2½ cups elderflowers, after stems cut off,
   lightly pressed into a jug
1 gallon plus 3 cups boiling water
3 lb (6¾ cups) sugar
2 lemons
yeast and nutrient, according to the pack instructions (see page 29)**

1. Put the elderflowers in a large preserving pan and add the water.
2. Add the sugar, and grated rind and juice of the lemons. Stir well.
3. Cool until under 86°F, then add the yeast and nutrient.
4. Cover tightly with muslin and leave to ferment somewhere warm for 4 days.
5. Strain through muslin into a sterilized demijohn, put in a bung and air lock and leave to ferment. When the fermentation has finished and the wine is clear, rack off the lees (see page 30) into a second sterilized demijohn and leave for 6 weeks. Then rack again, and bottle.

＊ *Elderflower Wine must always be served cool, and makes an aromatic, refreshing aperitif, similar to a light French or Italian white wine.*

＊ *Try matching this wine with white fish or seafood dishes.*

Dandelion Wine

Makes 1 gallon
plus 3 cups

Drink within
3 months of bottling

This is often the first wine to be made each spring from fresh ingredients. British tradition dictates picking dandelion flowers on St George's Day, April 23, but I've made dandelion wine earlier and then as late as the first half of May. One of my neighbors makes a rich, dark, long-aged version of this by using the full heads of dandelions and keeping it in demijohns for years, but this is my version: using only the petals to make a light, pale, dry white wine for drinking early. It tastes like a simple but refreshing Italian Soave or Frascati.

2 quarts dandelion petals
1 gallon plus 3 cups boiling water
rind and juice of 1 orange
rind and juice of 2 lemons
2¼ lb (about 5 cups) superfine sugar, preferably brewer's sugar (see page 29)
yeast and nutrient, according to pack instructions (see page 29)

1. Pick 2 large plastic bags full of dandelions, cutting them just below the head. Sort through them and shake to remove any insects. Using sharp scissors, cut away the green sappy part of each head, leaving only the petals and a little bit of the white inner head. Do this until you have just over 2 quarts' worth of petals when packed lightly into a measuring jug.
2. Put the flowers into a preserving pan or clean bucket. Add a boiling water, then the rind of the orange and lemons. Stir, cover, and leave for 4 hours to steep.
3. Add the sugar and the juice of the fruit. Stir until the sugar dissolves.
4. Cool to under 86°F, then strain through a fine muslin bag into another pan, squeezing the bag to get as much flavor out as possible.
5. Add yeast and nutrient to the liquid and pour into a sterilized demijohn. Put in a bung and air lock and leave to ferment for several weeks. Rack off (see page 30) and bottle.

* *Dandelions have a sticky sap that stains the skin, so use gloves when cutting off the petals.*
* *This wine is light, dry and delicate, and makes a good summer white. Serve well-chilled as a perfect partner for salads, tomatoes, white fish, and shrimp.*

Rose Petal Drink

*Makes about
2 quarts*

*Enjoy on the day
it's made, since it
doesn't keep well
and the fragrance
is soon lost*

The scent and color of rose petals can be rather elusive when making drinks. I favor "soft" rose drinks over fermented, as I think they capture the essence of the fresh flower best: delicate and lightly perfumed and unmistakably made from this wonderful bloom. This recipe comes from Azerbaijan. Make it with dark-red petals to get a lovely rich color.

petals from 4–5 large roses
2 quarts water
splash of lemon juice, to taste
3 tbsp superfine sugar

1. Rinse the rose petals gently and dry them on paper towels.
2. Bring the water to a boil in a large pan, then turn off the heat and add the petals and lemon juice. Stir.
3. Let the mixture stand for 6–8 hours. Strain and discard the petals.
4. Add the sugar and stir until dissolved. (Heat the liquid just a little bit if the sugar doesn't dissolve easily.) Stir and chill.
5. Serve this in a clear glass jug to show off the color. Add ice and float a few petals on the surface to garnish.

✳ *This delicate drink will be overwhelmed by rich or over-sweet food, but small, light savory snacks or elegant, simple cakes and cookies work well with it.*

✳ *Use only unsprayed rose petals. Even after washing, petals that have been sprayed with pesticides might harbor nasty residues. Never use bought roses for the same reason. You can use wild rose petals, but since these are smaller you'll need a lot of them! They also tend to have a lighter perfume than garden roses.*

✳ *Damask roses impart the strongest perfume to drinks.*

✳ *Try a simple tea version by covering petals from 8–10 large roses with 4¼ cups of water and bring slowly to a boil. Simmer for a few minutes, strain into 6 teacups, and add honey to taste.*

Lavender Lemonade

Makes 1½ quarts

*Store in the fridge
and drink within
a day or so; this
is best made in
small quantities*

This soft drink is one of my firm favorites. It's easy, quick, impressive—and kids love it, too. The first time I made it I was bewitched by the fragrance of steeped lavender that stole through the house. And by the fact that the liquid turns pink only when you add the lemons (why, I couldn't say). Make it from flowers that have "turned the corner" (are semi-dried) in high summer, or from dried blooms whenever you like.

about 1 tbsp lavender heads
2¼ cups boiling water
5½ oz (about ¾ cup) sugar
5 cups cold water
5 ripe lemons

1. Shake the lavender gently to remove any insects.
2. Put the flower heads into a saucepan and pour add the boiling water. Bring to a boil again and simmer for a minute or two.
3. Turn off the heat and leave for 10 minutes to steep. Strain.
4. Add the sugar and stir to dissolve. Add the cold water.
5. Squeeze the lemons directly into the pan (watch it turn pink!), then strain again to get rid of any lemon seeds or pith.
6. Taste to see how concentrated the flavor is. When serving, add more water to dilute according to taste.

* *Serve in a clear glass jug to make the most of the pretty color. Add plenty of ice and stir with thick, dried lavender stalks for effect.*

* *This is an immensely refreshing hot-weather drink, especially on a heavy, humid, late summer day.*

* *Add a shot of vodka for a great instant cocktail. Even better, mix lavender lemonade and vodka in a cocktail shaker with ice, shake, then strain into martini glasses for an elegant scented aperitif.*

Lavender Vodka

Makes 1½ pints

*At its best within
a couple of weeks
of making*

As easy as it gets. The distinctive scent of lavender appears quickly and is retained well in the spirit. But remove the lavender stalks after two weeks; otherwise the vodka turns brown and starts to taste woody—not good!

15–20 dried lavender flower heads, long stalks still attached
1½ pints good-quality vodka (unflavored)

1. Don't wash the lavender; just shake it gently to remove any insects.
2. Now simply pour a little vodka into a jug and set aside, then push the lavender stalks down into the bottle, head first.
3. Top up with the reserved vodka (keeping any amount leftover in another bottle or jar for topping up later), seal again, and turn several times.
4. Turn every day or so for 14 days, then take lid off and check. The liquid should have a floral scent. Remove the lavender. Top up with more reserved vodka, reseal, and store in a cool, dark place.

* *Serve ice-cold in shot glasses in hot weather.*
* *Consider making this in half-bottle quantities using 8–9 lavender stalks, since a full bottle might be too much to drink quickly! This vodka doesn't last as well as some spirit infusions (see also pages 122–31).*
* *This is a "dry" vodka, which works best in my opinion, although you could always make a sweet version by adding sugar (approximately 3–4 tsp) at the initial steeping stage.*
* *Serve with fruity, cool desserts such as sorbets, granitas, or rosewater panna cotta.*

SUMMER FRUIT DRINKS

I love the plump, juicy fruit of summer just as much for making into drinks as for eating. In a good year, fruit such as blackcurrants, gooseberries and plums can produce a sudden and sensational surplus, so I welcome as many ideas as possible for using them. Here is a wide-ranging selection of drinks to make from the high-summer harvests, including soft-fruit cordial for all the family and some tempting wines.

An English summer doesn't often last long, and I miss these crops when it's over every year. For ideas on making these drinks out of season from frozen, canned or bought fruit (and why not?), see page 14.

Blackcurrant Cordial

*Makes approx.
1½ pints*

*Keeps well in the
refrigerator for
up to 6 weeks*

It's amazing how expensive blackcurrants are. Although they're rare in the US. it's much cheaper to grow your own if you can. Blackcurrants need picking all at once, however, usually in a rush before the birds get them. No matter how you get hold of them, though, try making this vitamin-C-packed cordial. Children love it.

Wear an old apron and rubber gloves while dealing with blackcurrants if you don't want to end up with purple clothes and fingers. It's hard to imagine anyone taking a dislike to this drink, so make plenty to last you through the year (see freezing tip below). Like all cordials, dilute it with water, either still or sparkling, to taste.

1¾ lb blackcurrants
1 lb 2 oz (2½ cups) superfine sugar
2¼ cups water
juice of 2 lemons

1. Work through the blackcurrants, destalking as many as possible. Wash them well.
2. Put the fruit, sugar and water in a large saucepan and heat slowly and gently, stirring to dissolve the sugar.
3. Bring the pan to a very gentle simmer for 5 minutes. Do not boil vigorously or for any longer or the fresh taste of the fruit might be lost. It's not supposed to turn into jam!
4. Add the lemon juice, stirring well. Simmer gently for another 5 minutes, turn off the heat, cover, and leave to cool.
5. Once cool, either sieve it twice or pass it through fine muslin. Pour into sterilized bottles.

* *This freezes well, so I always split the batch into several small plastic bottles and freeze some. Leave a bit of space at the top of each bottle you intend to freeze; liquid expands during freezing.*
* *Freeze the cordial as individual ice cubes and pop them into glasses of cold water to keep kids happily hydrated in summer.*
* *Experiment with different variations on this theme: for example, use this recipe but replace some blackcurrants with 30 percent raspberries or redcurrants, or a mix of 15 percent of each.*
* *Mix with ginger ale for a fun, fizzy, slightly peppery drink.*
* *Dilute with sparkling water and a lime slice for kids' "mocktails," or splash into cold, dry, sparkling wine for a less powerful version of Kir Royale for grown-ups.*
* *Reduce the cordial further to make a delicious sauce for game and duck, or to pour over sorbet, ice cream, cheesecake, and meringue.*

Strawberry Wine

*Makes 1 gallon
plus 3 cups*

*Store in a cool,
dark place*

*Best at about
4–6 months*

Ahh, strawberries. Their scent and juicy flesh are so redolent of summer days that I don't blame anyone for thinking they would rather simply eat fresh strawberries and never cook or preserve them, let alone make wine from them. But then I would tell them that strawberry wine is a wonderful drink. It's so easy, and as that unmistakable sweet perfume rises and the bright-red froth foams, it becomes a joy to make.

A delectable rosé hue, it delivers all the natural flavor of this glorious fruit. My latest batch was slightly off-dry, juicy, and addictive, yet with crisp acidity to balance it. After months of fermenting and aging, the wine continues to give off the tempting aroma of fresh fruit. This is one of the very best fruit wines. A waste of good berries? No way!

1 gallon boiling water
4 lb strawberries, preferably local
2 lb (4½ cups) sugar
½ tbsp critic acid
yeast and nutrient, according to the pack instructions (see page 29)
rind and juice of 2 lemons

1. Bring the water to a boil point in a large preserving pan. Meanwhile, wash and roughly hull the strawberries. Add the fruit to the boiling water and simmer for 10 minutes. Stir, but be careful not to mash up the berries.
2. Turn off the heat, add the sugar, citric acid, yeast and nutrient, and pared rind and juice of the lemons. Stir, cover securely (strawberry juice attracts flies!), and leave overnight to steep and cool.
3. The next day, strain into a sterilized demijohn, add the yeast and nutrient, and fit an air lock and bung. Rest the demijohn in a bucket or bathtub in case it froths over.
4. After fermentation, which is likely to be vigorous and relatively quick (especially in hot weather), rack off (see page 30) and bottle.

* *Store in a dark place if you want to retain the pink color. Consider using a dark-glass demijohn and eventually dark-glass bottles, although the latter seems a shame when pink wine looks so pretty.*
* *This isn't a wine to keep for too long, because the fresh, fruity aroma and flavor will start to fade. Wine made in July is rewarded by a cool glass in November: a welcome memory of summer on a dark, cold night.*
* *This is not a real sweet or dessert wine so don't drink it with a rich dessert. Its off-dry flavor and juicy qualities work well with a crisp, fresh, fruit salad.*

Gooseberry Wine

*Makes 1 gallon
plus 3 cups*

*Keeps best in the
refrigerator, for
up to a year*

Use this recipe with gooseberries of any hue. It makes a superb fruit wine, with good, crisp acidity and plenty of bright, fruity aroma and flavor for balance. During an exceptionally hot early summer one year, I ended up with an overload of really ripe, bright-cerise gooseberries. Six months later, the resulting wine was even tastier, and the candy-pink color added an extra appeal.

Pink gooseberry wine at six months old is like a dry, refreshing, young European rosé; it develops into a delightfully refreshing, elegant, dry rosé that's almost Provençal in style. Green gooseberry wine is more akin to a light, dry French white.

Note: you don't need citric acid or lemons here; gooseberries are sour enough, although the end result is surprisingly well-balanced. In my opinion this is one of the most successful of the fruit wines.

4 lb gooseberries, preferably very ripe and pink
pinch of pectic enzyme (see page 29)
yeast and nutrient, according to the pack instructions (see page 29)
1 gallon plus 3 cups cold water
3 lb (6¾ cups) brewer's sugar (see page 29)

1. Hull the gooseberries and wash them well. Place the fruit in a large, clean pan or bucket and mash it with a potato masher. Add the enzyme, yeast and nutrient, and stir.
2. Add the cold water, stir, and cover loosely but well with clean linen.
3. Leave to stand for 3 days, stirring occasionally.
4. Strain through muslin into another clean container, add the sugar, and stir well until completely dissolved.
5. Pour into a sterilized demijohn and fit an air lock and bung.
6. After fermentation (probably long and slow) leave to age in the demijohn for several more weeks, then rack off the small amount of sediment, and bottle (see page 34).

* *Discard the solid parts of gooseberry after straining. Because they'll have traces of yeast, nutrient and enzyme on them, they can't be used in cooking.*
* *Try this wine with simple white fish or trout; its delicate flavor matches them well.*

Plum Wine

Makes 1 gallon plus 3 cups

Keeps for up to a year

Depending on where you live, plums can seem like a precious commodity, especially if you're paying for decent ones. But if you have plum trees, you have an almost annual surplus, and it's quite a task to harvest all the plums before they become inedible windfalls, bruised and attracting wasps. Wine might be a welcome solution. This makes a really appealing, bright-cerise, fresh and fruity rosé, very much in the style of a dry French or Spanish pink. I make it with Victoria plums, but there's no reason you can't use other varieties.

5 lb ripe plums
1 gallon plus 3 cups water
pectic enzyme, according to the pack instructions (see page 29)
3 lb 5 oz (about 7 cups) sugar
yeast and nutrient, according to the pack instructions (see page 29)

1. Wash the plums and discard the any parts that are rotten, split, or moldy.
2. Cut them into large pieces, retaining the stones, put into a large, clean container and bruise them well with a potato masher or the back of a large metal spoon.
3. Boil 2 quarts of the water and pour it over the crushed plum pieces. Cover well and leave for several hours to steep.
4. Now add the rest of the (cold) water, and the pectic enzyme. Cover again and leave to macerate for 3 days.
5. Strain through muslin into a preserving pan and heat gently, adding the sugar and stirring until it dissolves (you shouldn't have to boil it).
6. Allow this liquor to cool to under 86°F, then add the yeast and nutrient.
7. Pour into a sterilized demijohn and fit a bung and air lock. After fermentation you might need to rack this wine more than once to get rid of all the sediment (see page 30).

✱ *Drink this by itself, lightly chilled, or it's delicious with cold meats—especially chicken, turkey and pork—or mild cheeses.*
✱ *Remove the stones from the leftover plum pieces, and use the latter in several ways:*
    * *mulled plum jam, using red wine, port, spices, and citrus peel*
    * *other preserves or chutneys*
    * *fruit compotes*
    * *fruitcakes*

Rhubarb Wine

Makes 1 gallon plus 3 cups

Drink up within 6 months

Some homemade wines, however good, don't taste very strongly of the fruit that was used to make them. But this one does—maybe because, technically, it's not a fruit. So if you don't like rhubarb, be warned! I always have an abundance of rhubarb in early summer. Once the freezer is crammed with chopped stalks, I make a demijohn or two of this wine, which has a distinctive, very light spritz after bottling for the first few months. Expect high acidity (a welcome, refreshing quality in my opinion) and a slightly earthy, apple-core tone (a bit like cava).

3 lb rhubarb
1 gallon plus 3 cups boiling water
3 lb (6¾ cups) sugar
rind and juice of 1 lemon
yeast and nutrient, according to the pack instructions (see page 29)

1. Cut the rhubarb into pieces approximately 1¼–2 inches long, discarding the stumpy roots and very green tops of each stalk. Wash the pieces thoroughly.
2. Put the fruit in a large preserving pan or clean bucket and pour in all the boiling water. Don't heat it up again; just stir and allow it to steep for 20–30 minutes, by which time the stalks should have softened.
3. Press and bruise the fruit in the liquid using a potato masher or the back of a large metal spoon; you're aiming to squash it and extract plenty of juice. Keep mashing until the liquid is stained pink and the rhubarb is crushed a little, but not pulped.
4. Add the sugar and the pared peel and juice of the lemon. Stir well, cover loosely and leave to cool overnight.
5. Strain through fine muslin into a sterilized demijohn, adding the yeast and nutrient. Fit a bung and air lock.
6. After fermentation, rack off and bottle (see pages 30 and 34).

✱ *A delicious wine for late summer, this makes a great, palate-cleansing aperitif.*
✱ *This is a perfect base for homemade Kir, mixed with Crème de Cassis or Blackcurrant Cordial (see pages 62 or 54), since it has the high-acid kick required to offset the sweet cassis.*
✱ *Use the rhubarb and lemon left in the muslin to make preserves, or add a little to a pan of stewed rhubarb for extra concentration and flavor. Remember: it's already sweetened.*
✱ *Serve the wine with seafood, especially cold shrimp, crab, and lobster.*

Raspberry Gin

Makes 1 quart

*Will keep and
improves with age
(see tip below)*

A wonderful aromatic gin infusion, and one that is so much better if you follow all the tips given below. The main thing is to use good-quality, medium-ripe fruit, and no pale or green berries, overripe or bruised ones. Remember that raspberries are at their best for only a day or two, so pick or buy and use them quickly and with care.

7 oz (about 1½ cups) raspberries
6 oz (¾ cup) sugar
1 quart gin

1. Wash the raspberries thoroughly just before using; dry as much as possible and discard any damaged fruit.
2. Place the fruit in a 1-quart mason jar and sprinkle the sugar on top. Fill the jar right up with the gin.
3. Seal and shake gently until the sugar is nearly dissolved, then store for several weeks, turning every now and then. Keep in a dark cupboard and drink only after 10 weeks.

* *Raspberry Gin improves with age, so "cellar" some for a year or two if you have the patience, noting any changes and the optimum stage for drinking your version.*

* *It's a good idea to keep it somewhere dark. This helps retain the spirit's pretty deep-pink color.*

* *Raspberry Gin should be somewhat sweet, not cloying, and have a fresh aroma. When you first taste it, add a little more sugar if you think the infusion needs it. It's a good idea to taste after a few weeks to measure this, and you can add a little more gin to top it up at this stage.*

* *Shake in a cocktail shaker with a dash of dry vermouth, a splash of plain gin, and plenty of ice, then strain into a martini glass for a mouth-watering summer cocktail.*

Crème de Cassis

*Makes approximately
2½ quarts*

*Best enjoyed after
12 months maturing,
stored in a cool,
dark place*

For such a highly regarded, stylish drink, crème de cassis is surprisingly easy to make, provided you use decent red wine. Many beautiful cassis concoctions have been ruined by the addition of a bottle of rough red, or old, oxidized wine, so make sure you open fresh bottles for this job. Ripe, fruity reds are best: California Merlot, red Zinfandel, or southern French Grenache.

Note: this recipe is very similar to that for Crème de Mure on page 68, but cassis is more acidic, with a tangy, fresh lift on the finish.

3 lb 5 oz blackcurrants
2 quarts red wine
3 lb 5 oz (about 7 cups) sugar, possibly more to taste
1½ pints vodka (unflavored)

1. Wash the blackcurrants well, then work through them using a pair of small, sharp scissors, cutting off any tops and stems. Put them in a large preserving pan and crush them with a potato masher until all the berries burst and there's plenty of juice.
2. Pour the red wine over the top and stir well. Cover and leave to steep for 48 hours, stirring from time to time and covering again.
3. Strain through a muslin bag into a sterilized container. This can take some time, so consider hanging up the bag overnight (perhaps on the back of a chair) with the container underneath. Squeeze the bag at the end to get out the last of the liquid (wear rubber gloves!).
4. Rinse the original pan and pour the juice back in, now adding the sugar. Stir well. Heat up gently, still stirring, until the sugar has dissolved and the liquid is very hot but not quite boiling. Leave at just under simmering point to reduce until the liquid thickens and turns slightly more syrupy; this may take an hour or more. Stir from time to time.
5. Taste your liqueur, adding more sugar if you think it needs it for flavor and texture; stir the sugar to dissolve it if you've added more. Leave to cool.
6. Add the spirit, stir well, then pour into sterilized bottles.

* *Crème de Cassis also creates two traditional party classics: Kir and Kir Royale.*
    * *For a classic Kir: splash a small amount of Crème de Cassis in the bottom of a wine glass and top up with cold Aligoté (a grape from Burgundy) white wine, or use another dry, unoaked white such as Muscadet.*
    * *For Kir Royale: splash 1 tbsp Crème de Cassis into the bottom of a tall Champagne flute, then top up with chilled dry fizz, preferably Crémant de Bourgogne or even Champagne if you're feeling extravagant.*

* *Make a luxurious sauce for roast duck or goose with poultry stock, blackcurrants, and a knob of butter, adding a spoonful or two of Crème de Cassis, then heating it.*

* *Follow the French example and pour Crème de Cassis on ripe melons, or spoon it over poached pears served with vanilla ice cream.*

WILD DRINKS

To be honest, this is my very favorite part of the book. It gets
to the heart of why I started making my own drinks. Every fall I saw
an abundance of wild fruit covering the bushes and trees, yet aside
from the obvious trips to collect blackberries for desserts and jams,
I couldn't think of what else to do with any of it. Now I know, and
not only for blackberries, versatile little gems though they are, but
rosehips, sloes, the damsons that grow in our field, even certain
leaves and weeds.

So here's a good range of drinks made from a wild harvest. Sure,
certain ingredients come and go; the birds get a crop of blackberries,
or the best bush for rosehips disappears, or a patch of farmland is
claimed for an arable crop instead of wild sloe bushes. But there's
bound to be something you can harvest for drinks simply by making
a short walk from your front door (if you live in the country), or
by planning a longer trip out foraging (if you live in a city).
Provided, of course, that you don't trespass in the process, it will
be well worth the effort. And did I mention "free?"

Blackberry Cordial

Blackberry cordial works perfectly well, and it's a great way of using up a load of free wild fruit. But it lacks the zingy lift, the natural acidity, of blackcurrant cordial, and is more appealing when a sharper note is added, usually in the form of citrus-fruit juice (see tip below). I make this with ripe, juicy blackberries, heated in a pan with one-third as much water. Add sugar a little at a time (and keep tasting to avoid overloading this already sweet fruit). Simmer slowly until reduced by a third, then cool, strain, and bottle. It will keep for up to a month in the refrigerator.

* Dilute according to taste, adding a splash of orange or other citrus juice to add the necessary tang.

* I use this as the base for a non-alcoholic, warm Halloween brew, with added cloves, cinnamon, and slices of fruit, eye of newt optional. Kids love it.

Blackberry Wine

Makes 1 gallon plus 3 cups

Drink up within 6 months

This country wine uses up a lot of blackberries: great when they're abundant and the bushes are heavy with fruit. It makes a pale-red wine, almost in the style of a simple Beaujolais, Italian Bardolino, or Australian Tarrango. Using this recipe, the result is off-dry, fruity, and fresh. Serve very slightly chilled and drink as a refreshing aperitif or with savory snacks.

6 lb blackberries
1 gallon plus 3 cups boiling water
2 lb (4½ cups) sugar
juice and pared peel of 2 lemons
½ tbsp citric acid
yeast and nutrient, according to the pack instructions (see page 29)

1. Pick over the blackberries and pull off any stubborn stalks, then wash in cold water and shake until semi-dry in a colander, batch by batch.
2. Put all the berries in a large preserving pan or clean heatproof bucket and pour the boiling water over them. Bring to a gentle simmer for 10 minutes, then turn off the heat.
3. Add the sugar and stir until dissolved, then the juice and pared peel of the lemons and the citric acid. Cover and leave overnight to steep and gradually cool.
4. Strain through muslin into a sterile container, then add the yeast and nutrient. Stir well.
5. Pour into a demijohn, fixing an air lock and bung. Blackberry wine throws a lot of sediment so you may need to rack it off more than once after the fermentation has finished before bottling (see page 30).

* *This wine starts off a deep, inky, purple-red but lightens a lot during fermentation, even if it's kept in the dark. After a month's fermentation, expect a pale, ruby-red hue. The texture is light.*
* *The length and vigor of the fermentation will depend a great deal on the temperature of the room where the wine is kept (see also page 30).*
* *A good wine to sip lightly chilled with cold meats: a plate of salami, chorizo and ham with a few tomatoes on the side is just perfect.*

Crème de Mure (Blackberry Liqueur)

*Makes approximately
2½ quarts*

*Drink within
6 weeks*

What a discovery: a gorgeous, seductive, sensationally sweet liqueur that's rich, deep-purple and wonderfully warming. A shot of homemade crème de mure makes a great autumnal digestif, but you can do so many other things with it: mix it into cocktails, pour it into a highball glass, use it in cooking…

Blackberries are available free for many of us, so this is a clever alternative to crème de cassis if you don't grow or have access to blackcurrants. But don't think of this liqueur as a "poor relation" to cassis; it has a wonderful flavor all its own. In fact, I know many people who prefer this blackberry version.

Now for the downside: blackberry juice (and even more so, the red-wine-soused blackberry liqueur) stains terribly, so watch out. Mash up the fruit in a really big pan or bucket that can easily take the load—or be sure to wear black!

3 lb 5 oz ripe blackberries
2 quarts red wine
2¼ lb (about 5 cups) sugar, possibly more to taste
1½ pints brandy or vodka (unflavored)

1. Pick over the blackberries, carefully removing the stalks, bits of leaves or twigs. Discard any very bruised or rotten berries. Wash them, drain in a colander, then put them in a very large preserving pan or clean, heatproof, food-grade bucket.
2. Crush the fruit well with a potato masher or use an electric hand blender. Pour in the red wine and stir well. Cover and leave to steep for 48 hours, stirring from time to time.
3. Strain through a muslin bag into a sterilized container, squeezing the bag to get most of the liquid out (you might want to wear rubber gloves for this).
4. Rinse the original pan and pour the juice back in, then add the sugar. Stir well. Heat up gently, still stirring, until the sugar has dissolved and the liquid is very hot, but not boiling. Leave it at just under simmering until the liquid thickens and turns slightly syrupy. This may take an hour or more. Stir occasionally.
5. Taste, and add more sugar if you think it's needed for flavor and texture. Leave to cool.
6. Add the brandy or vodka, stir well, and pour into sterilized bottles.

* *Use a good-quality, freshly opened red wine to make this liqueur. Cheap red won't do! A fruity, medium-bodied style is just right.*
* *Which spirit should you use? Vodka is cheapest and works fine, but for a deluxe version, opt for premium French brandy for its richer, fruity notes. Armagnac is especially good.*
* *Drink this fairly quickly after making it because it doesn't store as well as crème de cassis, and will lose its fresh aroma and fruity edge, possibly because of its relatively low acidity.*
* *Crème de mure is very, very good with duck. Simmer the liqueur further to make it thicker and more syrupy and serve with rare duck breast.*
* *It's also great for pouring over ice cream, chocolate cake, and pie—even vanilla cheesecake.*

Blackberry Whiskey

Makes 1 quart

*Will keep for a year
and possibly longer,
after the blackberries
are removed*

This is for the grown-ups on Halloween—indeed, all through the chillier months, and especially when there may be a head cold lurking. It's a warming, fruity, sweet and slightly spicy shot, where the fruit takes away the more fiery, peppery edge of the whiskey.

I've tried various spirit bases for a blackberry infusion; they all work fine, and aren't hugely distinctive, so feel free to use vodka or gin if you prefer. But the wood-spice of Scotch seems particularly well-suited to blackberries, and for that matter, to the sometimes dreary period between October and Christmas.

1 lb 5 oz ripe blackberries
10½ oz (about 1¼ cups) sugar
1 quart Scotch whiskey

1. Pick over the blackberries, removing any stalks and leaves. Wash carefully, drain, then dab with paper towels until dry.
2. Pack the fruit into a large, sterilized mason jar (or two smaller ones) filling it about two-thirds full. Add all the sugar, then fill to the brim with whiskey. Seal the jar and turn it several times to mix.
3. Turn regularly during the next 24 hours until the sugar has dissolved.
4. This will be ready to drink after 3 weeks, although it's better if kept longer. Remove the blackberries after 6 weeks if you haven't drunk it all, though, to be certain that no rotten or woody flavors start to creep in.

✱ *Don't use a very smoky, peaty Islay whiskey for this; it tastes too strong for the blackberries, and anyway, it would be a shame to waste it on an infusion! Go for a decent, reasonably priced blended Scotch.*

✱ *Serve at room temperature. This winter warmer isn't meant to be chilled.*

✱ *Try adding a splash to fruit compotes or red-berry pies and desserts (for adults only).*

Elderberry Wine

Makes 1 gallon
plus 3 cups

Enjoy within
2–6 months, as
this is when it
tastes most lively
and vibrantly fruity

Elderflower drinks are tempting (see pages 42–45), but please leave enough blossom behind in order to get a decent crop of elderberries, too, in the fall. They make one of the very best "country wines," and it's a free fruit that has very little other use, so once you see them ripening, pick 'em quick and start fermenting.

This is remarkably similar to a light, fresh, young red made from grapes: an Italian wine such as Bardolino or a young, simple Merlot. It's also aromatic, full of forest fruit, raisin, and berry flavors (and not just elderberries).

Go for the long-soak method to obtain as much extract, color, and fresh, fruity character as possible. The wine is on the medium-dry side rather than bone-dry; simply reduce the amount of sugar if you prefer a tarter finish.

3 lb 5 oz elderberries
1 gallon plus 3 cups boiling water
yeast and nutrient, according to the pack instructions (see page 29)
1 tsp citric acid (see page 29)
3 lb (6¾ cups) brewer's sugar (see page 29)

1. Strip the little purple berries off their stalks by using a small fork and dragging down the bunches. The berries should pop right off in 1 or 2 drags: a really quick and strangely satisfying process. Make sure that you end up with 3 lb 5 oz of berries.
2. Put the berries in a preserving pan and crush them evenly and thoroughly with a potato masher. Add the boiling water, stir, cover, and leave to cool.
3. Once the liquid has cooled to under 86°F, add the yeast and citric acid. Leave for 3 days, well-covered with a permeable cloth, and stir from time to time.
4. Put the sugar in a sterilized container. Strain the cool elderberry juice through a muslin bag directly onto the sugar. Stir until the sugar has dissolved, then pour into a sterilized demijohn and fix an air lock and bung. Keep in a warm, dark spot. Fermentation can be long and slow in this case, but after it has finally finished, rack off and bottle (see page 34), preferably in dark-glass bottles to retain the color of the wine.

✳ *Serve at room temperature, or very slightly chilled if you want to enhance the succulent tang.*
✳ *A good elderberry wine is so much like a light, young red wine made from grapes that you can apply exactly the same serving ideas to it, so match it with:*
  ✳ simple meat dishes like ham salads and other cold meats and sausages;
  ✳ mild cheeses, roasted root vegetables, or mushroom dishes, especially risotto;
  ✳ simple tomato- or meat-based pasta sauces.

Rosehip Syrup

It seems like rosehips are everywhere in the late fall and winter: in gardens, the woods, up the walls of the house and poking prettily out of hedges. You can always use them to make rosehip jelly, but I'll bet a cordial of hips, glowing orange and smelling surprisingly fruity, gets used up by the whole family more quickly and enthusiastically.

Rosehip syrup is said to contain more vitamin C than citrus fruit: another great reason to make the most of this free autumnal crop. This is a drink that was made extensively in Britain during rationing after World War II, but don't think of it as a "hard times" cordial; it's really delicious. And kids adore it.

**2 lb rosehips
2 quarts plus 1½ pints boiling water
3¾ cups hot water
1 lb (2¼ cups) sugar**

1. Trim the rosehips and wash them well (no need to dry them).
2. Mince the damp fruits thoroughly in a food processor or blender. You might need to add a little cold water to aid this process, since they're fairly sticky and bits can get caught in the blades.
3. Pour the 2 quarts plus 1½ pints of boiling water into a pan, add the minced fruit, bring back to a boil again, and cook for 1-2 minutes. Turn the heat off and leave for 15 minutes.
4. Strain through a muslin bag and retain the liquid, putting the pulp back into the pan. Add the 3¾ cups of hot water to the pulp and bring it to a boil again.
5. Turn off the heat and leave for 10 minutes this time.
6. Strain again, putting both batches of hot liquid together, and discard the pulp. Heat the liquid to simmering and cook until reduced by one-third.
7. Add the sugar, stir to dissolve, and simmer gently for a further 5 minutes.
8. Allow to cool, pour into sterilized bottles and seal. Dilute with water to taste. Most children will want it strong and sweet!

* *Rosehip syrup doesn't keep particularly well. It soon loses its fruity, fresh aroma and general appeal, and it may start to ferment after several weeks. Drink within two weeks, then make some more.*

* *This is naturally cloudy, and an attractive peachy-orange color.*

* *Sip it as a hot drink to ward off colds, adding a small piece of fresh (peeled) root ginger to your mug.*

* *Mix it with a little ginger liqueur for grown-ups.*

* *Pour over pancakes or waffles for breakfast. Rosehip syrup is also delectable reduced even more and poured over creamy vanilla panna cotta.*

Nettle Beer

*Makes 1 gallon
plus 3 cups*

*Takes time to mature
and mellow. Best
after 8 months'
bottle-age*

Should I wax lyrical about the joys of picking nettles? No, it's a fairly unpleasant job—even though a vengeful joy can be found in doing something useful with such a pernicious and painful weed. Once you've got your nettles back home, process them quickly. The scent of cooking nettles isn't terribly pleasant, but what I do find satisfying is turning the crop into an attractive, clear, sparkling beer. Eventually. Well, what else can you do with nettles, except make soup? This is a lot more fun.

2 lb young nettle tops
1 gallon plus 3 cups boiling water
1 lb (2¼ cups) sugar
1 tbsp tartaric acid
zest and juice of 2 lemons
1 tsp brewer's yeast (see page 29)
1 tsp citric acid (see page 29)

1. Wash the nettles and strain/shake off most of the water. Put them in a large pan and add the boiling water. Bring back to a simmer and cook for 15 minutes.
2. Pour the sugar and tartaric acid into another large pan. When the nettle mix has cooled a little, strain it directly onto the sugar and acid. Stir to dissolve.
3. Add the pared zest and juice of the lemons. Allow to cool, loosely covered, for several hours.
4. Once under 86°F, add the yeast and citric acid and stir.
5. Strain again, pour into a sterilized demijohn and fit an air lock.
6. Once the fermentation has settled down and nearly finished (this may take several weeks), rack off the beer into another sterilized demijohn, leaving behind the sediment.
7. Add a couple of teaspoons of superfine sugar to prime the beer, then stir and syphon it into flip-top bottles (see opposite and page 27). Handle with care: the second fermentation should give bubbles to the beer.
8. Store in a cool, shady place and leave for 8–12 months to mature.

* *In time, this recipe produces a nettle beer that tastes pleasantly grassy and off-dry, with a fruity, almost apple-like note.*
* *The second fermentation sometimes fails to take off. If this happens, add a little more sugar and a minute pinch of yeast to the bottle and reseal. Beware of exploding bottles; always look away when opening.*
* *Nettle beer is a welcome and thirst-quenching draught with a simple lunch of cheese, bread, and salad (hold the pickles: they kill the beer's delicate taste). It goes best with anything bready or yeasty, such as savory rolls, sandwiches, or pizzas.*

Oak Leaf Wine

Makes 1 gallon
plus 3 cups

Drink after 6 months,
although this keeps
for up to 2–3 years

Oak Leaf Wine is well worth a try, but it seems to vary in character from batch to batch. The main reason is the time of year you pick the leaves: young, bright-green leaves make a fresher, lighter wine, while late summer leaves deliver a richer, more tannic, nuttier style. Either way, this isn't a wine to make in a hurry. Leave it to ferment very slowly. It may bubble quietly for several months, so just leave it alone. Once fermented, keep in the demijohn. For a good year or so it will only improve, becoming more mellow and complex. The color is a beautiful pale gold, the aroma slightly grassy with an interesting note of spiced orange, and the flavor is rich, viscous, with a citrus-oil depth and a sweet but well-balanced finish. There's a (nice) note of sherry in there, and I can taste fresh wood, almost as if it has been aged in casks. The oaked quality strengthens with age; think traditional white Rioja. It's fascinating stuff. It seems almost magical that wine can be produced from the juice and tannins of a bunch of leaves—but it can.

1 gallon oak leaves when pressed down lightly in a measuring jug
2¼ lb (about 5 cups) sugar
1 gallon plus 3 cups boiling water
2 tsp citric acid (see page 29)
yeast and nutrient, according to the pack instructions (see page 29)

1. Wash the leaves carefully and pick them over, removing woody stalks and insects lurking on the backs or in folds. Throw out bad leaves and shake the rest semi-dry.
2. Put the sugar into a large preserving pan or clean bucket and add the boiling water, stirring until the sugar has dissolved.
3. Bring the liquid back to a boil, then reduce to a simmer. When simmering, throw in all the oak leaves, pressing them down until they're covered. Stir well and turn off the heat. Cover loosely and allow to infuse. Cool overnight.
4. A day later, squash the leaves down well using the back of large metal spoon in order to extract a little extra character. Strain into a demijohn. Add the citric acid, yeast and nutrient, and a little cold water to top up if needed.
5. Fix the air lock and bung and allow to ferment until clear, racking off at least once before bottling (see page 30).

* *This is a strong, sweet, fairly weighty wine. Very different to those made with a fruit base.*
* *For an interesting experiment, make two demijohns and try them at different stages over a long period.*

Sloe Gin

Makes 1½ pints

*At its best after
1 year*

The extraordinary bittersweet, almond-and-juniper flavor of sloe gin is unique: a classic wintertime drink. If you're lucky, you'll know where to find sloes (sometimes called sloe-berries) each fall, but if the hard, dusty-matt, purple-blue berries prove elusive, look for the white flowers of the blackthorn shrub in spring. Come late autumn, that's your sloe bush!

Tradition says to wait until after the first hard frost of the autumn to pick sloes in order to get the best flavor, but you can treat an early crop to an icy blast in the freezer instead. Put the berries in overnight, then take them out and bruise them as they defrost by bashing them with the back of a metal spoon. If you haven't frozen them, prick each berry with a needle to split the tough skin and release some juice (a rather enjoyable job, I find, and so do my children). The most important thing is to get sloe gin made at least six weeks before Christmas so that it will be ready, albeit in a youthful, exuberantly fruity style, for the festive season. Older sloe gin tastes more rounded, mellow, and even a little spicy.

1 lb sloes
1 lb (2¼ cups) sugar
1½ pints gin

1. Go through your crop, taking out any bruised, broken or marked sloes.
2. Freeze or prick the berries, as described above. Put them into a couple of medium-sized, sterilized flip-top bottles or mason jars, dividing them equally, then pour equal amounts of the sugar over them.
3. Fill the bottles with gin and seal. Shake gently to kick-start the sugar-dissolving process.
4. Turn the bottles every hour or so for the first day, then once a day for the first week, then do it whenever the desire takes you.
5. A wonderful pinkish-purple color will start to seep out of the sloes after a few days.
6. Leave for at least 6 weeks (preferably 10) before drinking (around Christmas). Sloe gin improves with age, so keep a bottle for next year, but remember to remove the sloes after 3 months.

* *To emphasize the nutty, kernel-like quality of the drink, add a few drops of almond essence to the gin when you first make it.*

* *You don't have to discard the sloes after extracting. "Slider" is made by adding the gin-soused sloes to good farmhouse hard cider, and leaving it for 6-8 weeks until the liquid tastes like apples and sloes with a hint of nuts. A great tradition from rural Devon, England.*

* *Dilute with sparkling water and a dash of lime juice for a longer, more refreshing drink in warmer weather. Or try a Sloe Gin Fizz: mix equal shots of plain gin, Sloe Gin, and lime juice, add a dash of sugar syrup and shake over ice. Strain into a tall tumbler and top up with cool soda water.*

* *A judicious splash of sloe gin gives an extra kick to autumnal fruit compotes, especially spiced red plums or a blackberry-based mix.*

Damson Gin

Makes 1½ pints

Best enjoyed at
6–10 weeks, but
will keep longer.

Just the same as the sloe recipe, but damsons yield a sweeter, more juicy, plum-like liqueur; not gloopy, but rich, with a fine balance of sweet and sour in the fruit, and without the bitter character of sloes. Also, the actual gin flavor is less obvious in the damson liqueur. Personally, I prefer damson; it's exquisite, although the fruit is much rarer here than sloes (and more jealously guarded!). I make this in September.

1 lb wild damsons
8 oz (1 cup) sugar
1½ pints gin

1. The damsons shouldn't need washing, but sort through and remove any bruised or rotten ones. Prick each damson 2 or 3 times with a needle.
2. Tip the fruit into a clean, sterilized jar (or jars); note that you'll have trouble stuffing them into a very narrow-necked bottle. Pour in the sugar and top up with the gin.
3. Seal and shake to encourage the sugar to start dissolving, then turn gently every few days for between 8 and 12 weeks before drinking. If you are going to keep it for more than 3 months, strain off the damsons.

* *Sweet and juicy, this is a delectable winter digestif.*

* *Try serving a small shot with full-flavored hard cheeses such as tangy farmhouse Cheddar.*

* *Splash some into a rich gravy for game meats, especially pheasant or venison.*

* *Don't discard the used damsons: remove the stones, chop, and stew them with sugar for use in sweet pies, or spoon over ice cream, or add them to a fresh lot for an extra kick to jam or jelly. Most of the alcohol in the gin-soaked fruit will cook off, but some gin-like flavor will linger.*

* *The fruit below is actually bullace, a thornless fruit that's sharp in taste but not bitter like sloes. If you happen to find these while foraging, try using them in place of sloes or damsons and make bullace gin.*

Quince Vodka

I challenge anyone not to like this. Quinces give vodka a yellow glow and a honeyed flavor. This is another drink that you make in fall to be ready by Christmas. What a great gift idea!

2 large quinces
2¼ cups vodka (unflavored)
7 oz (1 scant cup) golden superfine sugar

1. Wash and dry the quinces, then grate them, whole and unpeeled, using the coarse side of a grater. Use the entire fruit: core and all. As you grate, put batches into a mason jar and splash in a little vodka; otherwise the fruit will turn brown.
2. Work swiftly. Pile all the pieces into the jar, add the sugar, then fill the jar with the vodka.
3. Seal and turn gently to mix. Turn every day for 2 weeks, then occasionally for another 4 weeks. Strain after this period, discard the quince pieces and bottle the beautiful golden spirit.

* *This tastes very sweet and doesn't need any more sugar added at the end (as some recipes suggest).*
* *Delicious with a fresh fruit salad, or with a plate of preserved fruit (apricots, figs, dates), toasted hazelnuts, and pistachios.*
* *I've made this with decent windfalls, but inspect each quince carefully and discard any that are very bruised.*

CITRUS DRINKS

Why bother making your own drinks out of citrus fruit when there are so many to choose from on the supermarket shelves? Especially when you're bound to be buying the fruit, since you're hardly likely to grow large crops of oranges or lemons yourself? The answer is simple: because these citrus-fruit cordials are *so* good. They taste natural, juicy, and exuberantly tangy— just like the fresh, ripe fruit. How many supermarket products can you say that about?

Make sure you buy unwaxed fruit wherever possible and try to choose organic. It's important to give citrus fruit a good feel to make sure it's plump and ripe. If not, bring it home and ripen it on a warm windowsill, or, at a squeeze (sorry!), put it in the microwave for 30 seconds to bring out all those natural fruit juices. You don't need a fancy juicer or even a basic squeezer for these recipes; just stick a fork into one-half of any citrus fruit and twist the prongs around and around, pressing the skin as you go and collecting the juice in a large bowl.

Note: citric acid adds an extra tangy bite and acts as a preservative. I like it with lemon cordials, but not so much with the riper, more exotic flavors of mandarin orange and lime. But use it as you prefer.

Lemon Cordial

Makes 3¾ cups

*Keeps for up to
2 weeks in the
refrigerator, or
freeze it in small
plastic bottles*

There are numerous recipes around for lemon cordial, but this is the best and it's fabulous: just the right balance between sweet and sour. It's my mother's recipe, and I've been drinking it for decades. Just the thing to get anyone started on making citrus cordials.

1 lemon
10 ½ oz (1½ cups) sugar
3¾ cups boiling water
2 tsp citric acid (see page 29)

1. Peel the lemon zest thinly, making sure you leave the white pith behind. Cut the peeled lemon in half.
2. Put the zest in a large glass or plastic jug and squeeze the juice from the peeled lemon halves over the top. Make sure the water is boiling.
3. Pour the sugar over the fruit and then pour in all the boiling water. Stir well until the sugar has dissolved.
4. Add the citric acid and stir well again. Cover and leave overnight to cool and steep.
5. Strain through a sieve and bottle. Dilute with water to taste.

* *To make lemonade, dilute to taste with chilled sparkling or soda water.*
* *Try this recipe with 2 or 3 limes to 1 lemon and a little less sugar and citric acid.*
* *Make up the concentrate in a glass jug with interesting additions such as bruised mint leaves (in summer), or ginger syrup from a jar of preserved stem ginger (in winter).*
* *Add ice cubes, mint sprigs, and slices of lemon and serve to party guests who don't want to drink alcohol It really beats supermarket lemonade.*
* *Try serving this ice-cold with a shot of good vodka or gin: amazingly refreshing!*

Pink Lemonade

Use the Lemon Cordial recipe above, but throw in a handful of ripe fresh raspberries when you add the sugar and boiling water. These add a pink glow to the cordial and give it a juicy, red-berry dimension. Top up with chilled sparkling water or soda.

Lemon Barley

Use the Lemon Cordial recipe above, but when the cordial is ready to leave overnight, simmer half a cup of pearl barley for 5 minutes, drain, rinse it thoroughly, then add it to the mix to steep before straining. This gives it a more complex, slightly malty quality.

Mandarin Orange and Lime Cordial

Makes 1¼ cups

*Keeps for up to
2 weeks in the
refrigerator, or
freeze it in small
plastic bottles*

Tried and tested, this aromatic, vivacious mix is the most popular (after pure lemon)
of all the citrus-fruit cordials I make for my children and adult friends. Try it only
when there are very big, juicy, ripe mandarin oranges available; it won't work well at all
with drier, tougher fruit.

6 large mandarin oranges
2 ripe limes
1¼ cups water
3½ oz (just under ½ cup) sugar

1. Halve and squeeze the fruit by hand (seeds, zest, and all) into a jug, then strain through
   a sieve or strainer into a medium-sized pan. Add the water.
2. Bring to a gentle simmer and keep it there, stirring occasionally, until reduced by a third.
3. Turn off the heat and add the sugar, stirring until dissolved. Allow to cool.
4. Skim any pithy froth off the top and keep in the refrigerator. Dilute with water to taste.

* *Freeze this in ice-cube trays, popping out a small amount at a time to add to drinks.*
* *Mix with cachaça or white rum and mint for an instant mojito with a burst of citrus-fruit flavor.*
* *Try this cordial with vegetarian stir-fries, mildly spiced shrimp, or dishes flavored with coriander.*

St Clements

Makes 1¼ cups

*Keeps for up to
2 weeks in the
refrigerator, or
freeze it in small
plastic bottles*

A classic duo of orange and lemon with a little grapefruit thrown in for good measure:
truly refreshing.

4 large, juicy oranges
1 lemon
1 grapefruit
1¼ cups water
1 tsp citric acid (see page 29)
4 oz (½ cup) sugar

1. Halve each piece of fruit and squeeze them all into a jug. Pass the juice through
   a sieve or strainer into a large pan.
2. Pour the water over the fruit juices and bring to a gentle simmer.
3. Add the sugar and citric acid and stir over a low heat until dissolved.
   Simmer until reduced by one-third. Allow to cool.
4. Store in the refrigerator. Dilute with water to taste.

* *Diluted, this cordial makes a refreshing breakfast drink (especially if you've run out of fresh juice), with
  flaky pastries and fresh fruit salad.*
* *Try it instead of orange juice for a twist on classic cocktails such as a Tequila Sunrise (with tequila
  and grenadine syrup), or a Big Easy (with Southern Comfort, Cointreau, and ginger ale).*
* *Makes a delicious, non-alcoholic partner for fresh seafood, from shrimp or scallops to clams.*

Pink Grapefruit and Pomegranate Cordial

Makes about 1 cup

Keeps for up to 2 weeks in the refrigerator, or freeze it in small plastic bottles

This is a gorgeous, rosy-hued cordial when diluted with cool, sparkling water. It's even better topped up with an icy, dry fizz such as cava or even Champagne.

Pink grapefruit can be a shade sweeter than white, so go easy on the sugar, or add more citric acid for extra zing. The addition of fresh, healthy pomegranate juice really makes this special: these two fruits have a natural affinity.

4 large, ripe, pink grapefruit
¾ cup plus 1 tbsp water
3 oz (¼ cup plus 2 tbsp) sugar
2 tsp citric acid (see page 29)
2 pomegranates

1. Halve the grapefruit and squeeze their juice into a large jug. Strain the juice into a large pan.
2. Add the water and bring to a gentle simmer.
3. Add the sugar and citric acid and stir over a low heat to dissolve. Simmer gently to reduce by at least one-third. Allow to cool.
4. Halve the two pomegranates, then pull out all the seeds from the centre with a fork. Mash the seeds coarsely to release the juice.
5. Strain and add the pomegranate juice to the grapefruit cordial. Stir well.
6. Store in the refrigerator, spooning off any froth that rises to the surface after the liquid cools. Dilute with water to taste.

＊ *The perfect brunch drink: it's delicious with eggs, toast, jam, and fresh fruit.*

＊ *This cordial is especially good when made with sparkling water or soda.*

＊ *For a more alcoholic version, add a splash of tequila and top up with cold sparkling wine.*

Lime, Ginger and Lemongrass Cordial

*Makes just over
1 pint (18 fl oz)*

*Keeps for up to
2 weeks in the
refrigerator, or
freeze it in small
plastic bottles*

This is something different: a scented, exotic cordial inspired by some of the bought ones that go so well with Eastern cuisines, especially Thai food. By now it shouldn't surprise you when I say that this homemade version tastes better.

10 lemongrass stalks
2 large pieces of fresh root ginger (approximately 2 x 1¼ inches)
peel and juice of 6 fresh, ripe limes
1 pint plus 1 tbsp boiling water
4 oz (½ cup) sugar

1. Trim the lemongrass stalks and peel off the roughest outer layers. Slice them lengthwise, then chop finely. Bruise the chopped pieces a little with a potato masher in a large bowl.
2. Peel the ginger and grate it roughly. Add it to the lemongrass.
3. Pare the rind thinly from the limes and put it in a large saucepan. Add the lemongrass and ginger mix and boiling water, followed by the juice of the limes.
4. Stir, heat, and simmer for a couple of minutes, then turn off the heat and add the sugar, stirring until it dissolves. Steep the hot mixture for 1 hour.
5. Strain through a muslin bag, squeezing the last drops of liquid out of the bag by hand to release as much flavor as possible.
6. Bottle and keep in the refrigerator. Dilute with water to taste.

✳ *For a sweeter version, add a large tablespoon (or even two, according to taste) of the syrup from a jar of preserved stem ginger to the final, cooled mix before bottling.*
✳ *Try this cordial with fragrant Thai chicken, seafood, and vegetable dishes that have coriander, lemongrass, and maybe coconut milk in the recipe.*

Limoncello

Makes 2 quarts

Keeps for years

How many drinks are this mouth-watering yet powerful, fresh-tasting yet long-lived? Or packed with tangy acidity, yet syrupy and thick, and are sipped after dinner as a digestif? At least, that's how they drink limoncello in southern Italy, especially along the Amalfi coast and in Sicily. Much as I'd like to be raising a glass there right now, you can conjure up the same intensely lemony liqueur at home very easily indeed.

peel and juice of 5 ripe lemons, plus 1 for decorating finished bottles
1 quart vodka (unflavored)
1 lb 10 oz (about 3 cups) sugar
1½ pints boiling water

1. Pare the rind thinly from the lemons, taking care to avoid the white pith.
   Divide the rind between 2 large, clean glass jars; 1-quart mason jars are perfect.
2. Pour the vodka over the lemon rind in the two jars, seal them, and turn them to mix.
3. Leave for 1 week, shaking the jars gently from time to time.
4. Put the sugar in a large heatproof bowl, add the boiling water and stir well to dissolve.
5. While the sugar syrup is still hot, add the vodka and lemon-rind mix. Stir, cover and leave for 1 week.
6. Strain and divide between the cleaned jars, and add a few fresh strips of rind from a new lemon to each jar to decorate. Seal and keep forever.

* *Classic limoncello is made with Sorrento lemons, but any good-quality unwaxed (and preferably organic) lemons will do.*

* *If drinking this as an after-dinner digestif, serve in shot glasses, chilling both glasses and limoncello well in advance.*

* *Dilute with sparkling water to make a gorgeous, zesty drink, adding the juice of one fresh lemon per four drinks for extra zing.*

* *This is a great cocktail ingredient. Use it to make limoncello martinis with equal parts vodka (unflavored) and limoncello, and a small dash of fresh lemon juice, all shaken over ice and strained into chilled martini glasses.*

* *Pour over pancakes and/or ice cream, or use it to make a grown-up lemon drizzle cake.*

ORCHARD DRINKS

Every fall I stare in wonder at the beautiful crops of apples and pears on the trees of southwest England, where I live. And then I can hardly believe it when some of this fabulous fruit is left to rot on the ground or to wither, even freeze, on the trees. OK, so we have a lot apples in this particular corner of the world, but surely someone must want to use this fruit?

Inexpensive supermarket apple juice is something we all take for granted, but when you think about it, a lot of the cheaper stuff made from concentrate doesn't actually taste that great. Press your own and I bet you'll start freezing it by the gallon. Cider (hard or non-alcoholic) is so simple to make. Why not give it a try? And apple wine is a must for anyone who has access to large amounts of orchard fruit. There's a real community feel to the apple-picking and pressing season around here. If you're lucky enough to live in apple country, find out who else may be picking and pressing in your vicinity, and get to the real "core" of these drinks.

Pressing apples and pears for juice

It's a fairly daunting, if enticing, sight: big baskets or sacks piled high with newly picked orchard fruit, some a little bruised, perhaps; some with leaves and twigs attached; even a pasting of mud and a few insects crawling around the edges. How on earth do you get fresh, thirst-quenching juice out of that? Teamwork helps. Working with others to crush works best: a press is expensive, so don't fork out for one before asking around (or even advertising locally) to find one you can borrow.

You'll no doubt be using whatever fruit varieties you can get your hands on: a mongrel mixture of sweet dessert varieties, crisp, tart cider apples, or a small proportion of crab apples. The latter are the best of all, so blend your batches of homegrown fruit.

Take a close look at the fruit and only wash any that really need it; muddy windfall apples and pears will need hosing down. Now the production line starts: work through the fruit, removing stalks and leaves, and cutting out and discarding any bruised, rotten or otherwise blemished parts (and give these to any nearby pigs). Then chop the apples or pears into chunks roughly, quartering any small fruit, and cutting larger ones into six or eight pieces. Don't bother removing the core and definitely never peel them. Work fairly quickly or the cut fruit will oxidize. While one or two people chop, others should push the pieces into the crusher. The crushed fruit (called "pomace") must be pressed swiftly and the precious liquid caught in clean buckets.

The result usually looks less than perfect—amber, dense, and cloudy—but homemade juice always tastes wonderful. Bursting with fresh flavor, with a slightly tannic, dry finish and incisive, crisp, mouth-watering acidity. You may decide to dilute the juice with water a little at this point. Either way, freeze any that you won't be drinking as juice or fermenting into cider as quickly as possible; I use sterilized plastic milk and juice cartons for this, leaving a little space for the liquid to expand on freezing. Make sure that the crusher is cleaned thoroughly. Ferment the juice sooner rather than later in order to preserve as much freshness in your hand-pressed orchard juice.

PS: I know some who use bought apple and pear juice to make cider and perry (fermented pear juice). If you must, try this using the best cloudy, fresh juice you can buy and follow the same recipes in this chapter, but it won't be nearly as good the home-pressed stuff—and you won't have nearly as much fun getting it!

Hard Apple Cider

*Makes 1 gallon
plus 3 cups*

*Keeps up to
12 months*

For the serious cider-maker there are plenty of books that will take you down the advanced route, suggesting particular apple varieties or blends of varieties, commenting on yeast strains, etc. But for the rest of us, hard cider couldn't be easier to make. It's simply fermented apple juice.

One important tip: take your newly pressed apple juice, taste it, and if you really think it needs sugar, add it. But most juices that have been made from a balanced mix of ripe, sweet, and acidic/bitter apples don't require more sweetening (and note that adding sugar could make your cider much stronger). I use the same type of yeast as for fruit wines, but you can buy special cider-yeast strains at home-brew suppliers if you prefer. Or why not make several demijohns of cider using different yeast strains and see which you like best?

**1 gallon plus 3 cups fresh apple juice: from a mix of sweet, acid, and
   bitter varieties**
yeast and nutrient, according to the pack instructions (see page 29)

1. Bring the apple juice to room temperature if it has been chilled.
2. Strain it through fine muslin or a sieve/strainer into a large, sterile container to remove any fine solid pieces. Add the yeast and nutrient.
3. Using a clean jug and a funnel, carefully pour the juice into a sterilized demijohn and fix an air lock and bung.
4. Treat just as you would a fruit wine, waiting until the fermentation has finished (or very nearly finished) before racking off once or twice (see page 30) and either maturing in the demijohn or bottling.

* *Cider fermentations seem to be very vigorous at first, so you might want to rest the demijohn in a plastic bucket or tray in case the froth spills over. Clean the air lock and bung after any such occurrence. Alternatively use a small glass placed upside down over the demijohn neck instead of an air lock and bung at first, but fit the latter after things calm down a little.*

* *Homemade hard cider tastes much, much better if left to ferment slowly through many weeks before maturing in the demijohn or bottle for several more months.*

* *Hard cider should be flat, not fizzy, like all traditional ciders. To make a sparkling version, see the method for making Perry on page 100.*

* *You'll have to use a hydrometer both before and after fermentation to find out the strength of your cider (see page 27), but if you don't, always assume it is on the strong side. It certainly isn't likely to be weak!*

* *Enjoy lightly chilled homemade hard cider with the classic English "ploughman's plate" of Cheddar cheese, crusty homemade bread and mild pickles. It also goes well with roast pork and apple sauce, sausages, cold chicken, and cheese-topped vegetable bakes.*

Apple Wine

*Makes 1 gallon
plus 3 cups*

Keeps up to 2 years

Don't avoid making apple wine because you're too wrapped up in making freshly pressed juice or hard cider. It is utterly delicious, and a great way of using up an abundance of apples. Choose only ripe fruit; using windfalls is also fine as long as you cut away any rotten or bruised parts. I'm sure you'll use whatever varieties are growing nearby, but some are better than others. This recipe makes a fairly dry style. Note the major difference between the method for Apple Wine and Hard Apple Cider: for this wine recipe, the apples are cooked first.

7¾ lb apples
1 gallon plus 3 cups water
2 lb 12 oz (about 5½ cups) sugar
1 tsp citric acid (see page 29)
yeast and nutrient, according to the pack instructions (see page 29)

1. Wash the apples well, snip off any stray stalks and leaves and cut away any brown or blemished pieces. Keep all healthy peel on the fruit.
2. Chop the fruit into small pieces.
3. Bring the water to the boil in a large preserving pan. Add the apple pieces, stir them in, and simmer gently for 15 minutes. Let the liquid cool for a few minutes until warm rather than hot.
4. Put the sugar and citric acid in another large, clean container and strain the warm liquid through muslin onto it, stirring until it has all dissolved. Let the liquid cool.
5. When cooled to under 86°F, add the yeast and nutrient. Use a funnel to pour the juice into a sterilized demijohn, fixing an air lock and bung.
6. When fermentation is finished, rack off the wine (see page 30) and bottle it (see below).

＊ *More acidic apples, even a small proportion of crab apples, add tang and tannins to the flavor of ordinary dessert apples.*

＊ *Use a normal wine yeast here. Home-brew author C.J.J. Berry says a "Sauternes" yeast is best of all; I use a Champagne yeast.*

＊ *This Apple Wine definitely improves with age and should be left before drinking for at least six months once bottled in a cool, dark place.*

Spiced Apple Cup

Makes just over
3 quarts

Best enjoyed on
the day it is made

This is perfect to keep spirits raised on a cold, windy autumn evening. I always make it after the troops have been pressing fruit in the yard as a "thank you," and I give it to chilly adults who are accompanying trick-or-treaters at Halloween, too. You can use apple juice for a non-alcoholic version or hard cider for an alcoholic version, adding a splash of apple brandy (use English apple brandy or Normandy's Calvados) for an even headier brew!

3 quarts fresh apple juice or hard cider
3 whole cloves
3 cinnamon sticks
2-inch knob of fresh root ginger, peeled and cut into thin slices
3 whole allspice berries
a little honey or soft brown sugar (optional, quantity as per your own taste)
juice of half a lemon
apple brandy (optional, for cider version only)
2 organic green and red dessert apples (for garnish)

1. Pour the apple juice or cider into a large pan and add all the spices.
2. Heat gently to just under simmering, stirring from time to time with a long-handled spoon and making sure the drink doesn't boil too hard. Taste from time to time, and if any spice seems especially strong, remove it and discard.
3. Add the honey or sugar, if using, little by little, tasting as you do so. Then do the same with the lemon juice and brandy, if using, until just the right balance has been found.
4. Quarter, core, and slice (but don't peel) the apples and drop the slices in for the last minute or two before serving.
5. Ladle into heatproof glass tumblers, making sure every drink has a clove or a piece of cinnamon and some apple slices. Serve immediately.

Pear Juice, Pear Wine and Perry

If you substitute pears for apples in the recipes in this chapter, you can easily make pear wine and perry. Use fairly ripe pears (not sour, hard ones) where possible, and in an ideal world, a good mix of tart and sweet varieties for a fine balance in the finished drink.

To make sparkling Perry, follow the recipe for Hard Apple Cider, using pears instead, then bottle the finished liquid in strong flip-top bottles, adding a little sugar to prime it (see page 29). Store and wait for the yeast to create bubbles, which will be trapped inside the bottle.

Be careful when opening in case pressure has built up. Always point the bottle away from your face (and anyone else's) and slowly ease off the top. Perry usually has subtle, delicate flavors and as such makes a delightful aperitif, or serve it with light savory snacks at a party, such as little cheese pastries.

Here's a refreshing, aromatic Pear and Elderflower Cocktail which can also be made as a refreshing "mocktail" for non-drinkers or children, simply by using chilled soda water instead of vodka.
1. Use 2 parts plain vodka and 2 parts fresh pear juice to 1 part homemade Elderflower Cordial concentrate, a splash of lime juice and a drop of sugar syrup (or runny honey).
2. Shake the vodka, pear juice and cordial in a classic cocktail shaker over ice.
3. Strain into tumblers over more ice, squeeze in the lime and sweeten to taste. For the soft version, leave out the vodka, shaking only the pear juice and cordial (or simply stir over ice in a jug), strain into tall glasses or cups filled with ice, and add the lime and sweet stuff.
4. Top up with plenty of soda.
5. Decorate both drinks with lime slices and mint leaves.

OTHER WINES AND GRAPE DRINKS

Homemade wine made from grapes? Fantastic! Except that there are thousands of reasonably cheap wines already crowding retailers' shelves, and many are just as palatable as anything you can make at home. I'd rather create my own wine and other drinks out of something different—preferably wild, free or surplus produce—and buy my fermented grape juice from a good retailer. If you buy a "wine kit" containing grape concentrate, by the way, it should come with very clear instructions. Instead, I make fresh grape juice from time to time when people give me homegrown grapes, and even occasionally, from bought ones. My children absolutely love it.

Would-be serious winemakers should look for a complete, in-depth manual to grape-growing and production. Here, instead, is my joyous take on grape juice, and two more recipes for country wines, which (usefully) can be made all year round, but tend to be my winter fermentations. This is because the key ingredients—parsnips, rice, and raisins—can be sourced easily in the colder months.

Parsnip Wine

Makes approximately
1 gallon plus 3 cups

Keeps for 1 year

There are countless recipes for making wine from vegetables, most of which aren't terribly tempting, but I'm glad I discovered parsnip wine. This sweet-tasting, cheap root vegetable, which you might have in your vegetable garden, makes a good base ingredient for wine at exactly the moment when many other raw ingredients are completely finished for the year. I make mine in November and it's ready by mid-January. The color of parsnip wine is an appealing creamy white; the flavor is medium-dry, rather honeyed, juicy, and full-bodied. If you like off-dry, fruity Riesling or Pinot Gris, then this is for you.

This (apparently "very old") wine is slightly adapted from *The Eynsham Cookbook*, a collection of recipes donated by villagers in my home town, west of Oxford, England.

5 lb parsnips
1 gallon plus 3 cups water
3 lb (6¾ cups) sugar
juice of 1 orange, strained
juice of 1 lemon, strained
yeast and nutrient, according to the pack instructions (see page 29)

1. Don't peel the parsnips; just wash them quickly, then trim them before finally chopping them into medium-sized chunks.
2. Put the parsnips in a large preserving pan and add the water. Bring to the boil.
3. Simmer for about 30 minutes, or until the parsnip pieces are soft.
4. Let the pan cool a bit until ready to handle, then strain through muslin or a fine sieve/strainer into a second large pan or clean bucket. Discard the parsnip pieces.
5. Add the sugar to the warm liquid, followed by the citrus-fruit juices.
6. Bring to a boil and simmer for 20 minutes.
7. Cool, adding yeast and nutrient when under 86°F. Pour into a sterilized demijohn, top up with cold water if necessary and fix an air lock and bung.
8. After several weeks' fermentation (this will depend on how cold the weather is), rack off and bottle.

* *Parsnip wine should be clear, with none of the creamy-cloudiness of the fermenting liquid. However, fermentation is slow, partly because it's usually made in the colder winter months. Patience is needed.*
* *Try a glass of parsnip wine with cold pork and chicken, or cheesy quiches and savory tarts, or a good cheese board and chunks of homemade bread.*

Red Grape Juice

Very roughly, you can expect just over ½ cup from 1 lb of grapes

Best enjoyed on the day it is made

Now this definitely is worth making on a small scale. My children absolutely adore it, and it's a wise alternative to wine for us, too, sometimes. It's something fun to do with the fruit of just one productive vine that you might have growing at home, either outside or (in cooler climates) in a greenhouse or conservatory. Here is the best method.

1. Make sure your grapes are ripe and taste sweet; keep trying one or two to check! Cut off the bunches using sharp clippers, collecting the fruit in small batches in a basket. Only pick the grapes close to the time you're going to make the juice; otherwise the fruit will start to taste less fresh pretty quickly.
2. Remove all the stalks, large and small, and discard any green, very hard, or old and moldy berries. Wash the grapes well in cold water and shake dry over the sink.
3. Now put the fruit into a pan (a big preserving pan if processing in bulk) and mash them with a potato masher, just enough to crush each berry and remove most of the juice, but not so roughly that you reduce everything to a complete mush and risk getting too many dry-tasting tannins from the skins.
4. Add enough water to come up 2 inches from the bottom of the pan, and simmer the grapes for 10 minutes, stirring from time to time to keep the skins from sticking to the bottom. Taste a little of the liquid and add sugar if required. Stir to dissolve.
5. Strain through a fine sieve/strainer or muslin bag and let cool. Dilute with cold sparkling water to taste.

* *You can follow exactly the same process with white grapes, although the results are less interesting and white juice lacks some of the health benefits of red.*
* *For rosé juice, crush the red grapes only a little and run off the lightly stained liquid quickly before the color turns fully red. The juice will taste fresh and fruity, but not as rich as red grape juice.*
* *Try mixing red grape juice with bought cranberry or pomegranate juice for a ruddy, rich, healthy glassful bursting with antioxidants.*
* *Drink as soon as it's made in the case of pink or white, and red within two hours; grape juice doesn't keep well—and it doesn't freeze well, either.*

Rice and Raisin Wine

*Makes approximately
1 gallon plus 3 cups*

Keeps for 6 months

This is another wine that can be made all year 'round, so it's a useful recipe to have when any seasonal crops are finished. I make it in winter so that the colder temperatures and lack of summer flies mean I don't worry too much about this being an "open" ferment. In fact, this is the only wine in the book that I allow to ferment in an open container for a long time, but since it isn't based on fresh fruit, I'm not aiming for bright, zesty flavors anyway. The results are can vary from batch to batch, probably because of the raisins. You should end up with a powerful, off-dry, amber-colored wine with the flavor of raisin still very much present, but (strangely) this is one recipe that fails from time to time. You could try boiling the raisins briefly after chopping and before using in the mix, or adopt a laid-back attitude to this one: it hardly costs much to give it a try, and when it does work, it is good.

**2¼ lb uncooked white rice
1 gallon plus 3 cups cold water
1¾ lb (about 3½ cups) sugar
1¾ lb raisins
juice of 1 orange
juice of 1 lemon
yeast and nutrient, according to the pack instructions (see page 29)**

1. Wash the rice well and leave it in a fine colander or sieve to drip until partially dry.
2. Pour a pint of the water into a medium-sized pan and bring it to a boil. Add all the sugar and stir until completely dissolved. Let the solution cool to lukewarm.
3. Chop the raisins very roughly with a large serrated knife in small batches on a chopping board. This releases some of the juices. Now put the raisins, rice, and citrus-fruit juices into a sterilized preserving pan or a large heatproof sterilized bucket.
4. Heat the remaining water until hand-hot.
5. Pour the sugar solution on the rice-and-raisin mix, add the rest of the water and stir well. Cover loosely (I use clean dishcloths) and let it cool until under 86°F.
6. Add the yeast and nutrient and give it a stir. Cover loosely again and leave in a warm place for 7 days to ferment.
7. Strain the fermenting mixture through a muslin bag, discard the solid pieces and pour the liquid into a demijohn, topping up with cold water if needed, and fixing an air lock and bung.
8. Once fermentation is over (and it should be relatively quick here) rack off the wine (see page 30) and bottle it.

HONEY AND GINGER DRINKS

Honey oozes up to the surface now and again throughout this book, especially as a natural sweetener for hot toddies and teas. It's a useful commodity, so it's great news when you find a source of honey nearby: especially as stocks are currently relatively scarce around the world. Try to smoke out any local beekeepers who will sell you honey, or perhaps even trade you some for a finished drink. Otherwise, bought honey is fine, but make sure you buy the clear, runny version, not the cloudy, solid stuff. And although cheaper brands are fine, if you trade up to top-quality honey the results will taste better for it.

As for ginger drinks, you might have noticed how much fresh ginger is used in this book. Homemade ginger drinks are among my very favorites. Ginger is fabulous. I love the unique, sweetened, juicy heat of the fresh root, and its lovely aroma when heated.

Both fresh and ground, ginger is cheap, easily sourced, and wonderfully versatile. See other uses for this useful ingredient on pages 87, 121 and 134. I especially like the fact that there are lots of non-alcoholic or very-low-alcohol drinks made from ginger as well as strong, heady ones, so you can tailor the drinks to suit children or drivers. Here are three drinks that put this humble, knobbly rhizome to good use.

Mead

*Makes 1 gallon
plus 3 cups*

*Keeps for several
years, but is best
drunk between
6–18 months
after fermentation*

To read some of the available information, you'd think mead was more difficult to make than any other drink in this book. That hasn't been my experience. I find mead pretty easy stuff. This is a straightforward, no-nonsense recipe for medium-dry mead adapted from a recipe in C.J.J. Berry's indispensable *First Steps in Winemaking*. It works. Enough said.

3 lb 5 oz honey
1 gallon plus 3 cups cold water
1 orange
1 lemon
yeast and nutrient, according to the pack instructions (see page 29)

1. Pour the honey into a large pan, add the water and heat to just under simmering point. Simmer for half an hour, stirring until the honey has dissolved. Skim off any froth, then pour into a clean container (a preserving pan or bucket) and let cool.
2. Once the liquid is cool, add the strained juice of the citrus fruits and an all-purpose wine yeast with nutrient.
3. Pour into a demijohn and fit an air lock and bung.
4. Wait until fermentation has finished. This may take longer than for fruit wines: about 2 months, depending on the weather (the colder it is, the longer it takes). Rack off the mead and bottle it.

✳ *Clover honey is said to be the very best for this, since it imparts a gentle, slightly grassy or floral note.*
✳ *Be careful not to boil the honey/water mixture too hard; otherwise it can lose its delicate aroma and flavor.*
✳ *You must use a wine yeast with nutrient here because honey doesn't provide enough food for the yeast.*
✳ *To make a sweeter mead, simply increase the quantity of honey used to 4 lb.*
✳ *Match medium-dry mead with mildly spicy food, a good cheese board and pork, ham and chicken.*

Metheglin (Spiced Mead)

The gentle flavor of honey marries well with aromatic spices. Just watch out that you don't overwhelm the honey with too much of a good thing: cloves, in particular.

Stick to the same basic recipe as above, but before step 1, add 2 tea bags and a muslin bag containing 4 cloves, 2 cinnamon sticks, 6 thin slices of fresh ginger root, 1 tbsp of caraway seeds and the pared and sliced rind of the orange to 1 gallon plus 3 cups of very hot water to steep before using.

Remove the tea bags after 5 minutes and the muslin bag after 30 minutes. Reheat the water until very hot before pouring it over the honey, then proceed to step 1 and follow the method as above.

* Spiced mead is irresistible when made into a hot toddy with a slice of apple, another clove and possibly a small splash of brandy or Calvados in each glass tumbler.

* Try it with mildly spiced food. Sounds obvious, but it works well with peppery Szechuan food and stir-fries with a little chilli pepper.

* Trivia for today: the Welsh word for metheglin (which sounds like a chemical) is meddeglyn, which I find more appealing, somehow.

Fruity Ginger Ale (non-alcoholic)

Makes 1 pint of concentrate

Keeps for a week or so in the refrigerator

This is a great one to whip up in a short time when you're expecting guests (young and old) and the weather is warm. It's popular with grown-ups, and goes down much better than boring orange juice when you need a soft drink to offer to drivers or other non-drinkers at a summer dinner party. You will find the concentrate very strong, sweet and peppery, so add plenty of lime and soda water to taste, particularly for children.

5½ oz fresh ginger root
2½ cups water
6¼ oz (about ¾ cup) sugar
soda water, dilute to taste (buy a big bottle and keep it in the refrigerator)
fresh limes, at least ½ per drink

1. Peel, then grate the ginger coarsely.
2. Heat 1¾ cups water in a medium-sized pan until boiling.
3. Add the ginger, reduce the heat, and simmer gently for 5 minutes.
   Remove from the heat, cover, and let the mixture steep for 30 minutes.
4. Strain through muslin or a fine-meshed sieve. Squeeze or press the ginger a little to remove more juice. Discard the ginger; most of the flavor will be gone.
5. Rinse the pan, add the rest of the water and bring it to a boil. Add the sugar, stirring to dissolve. Let the syrup cool.
6. Mix the ginger water with the sugar syrup. Keep it in the refrigerator and dilute to taste with cold soda water and a good squeeze of lime juice per glass. Add ice and a lime wedge to each drink.

* You can make a mildly spiced version by adding 3 allspice berries, 1 whole star anise and half a cinnamon stick to the ginger-and-water mix at the start of step 3.

* Use the very freshest ginger root you can find for this. It should snap, not bend, when you pull off a knob.

* This is a really refreshing drink, and it goes extremely well with spicy, savory food. "Instant" ginger beers like this are popular in West Africa and go well with African spicy stews, especially those based on root vegetables.

Ginger Beer

Some home-brewers swear by a ginger "plant"—a concentrate made with sugar, ground ginger, and yeast, which can be divided and used again and again—but I rarely bother with the rest of the "plant" after making just one batch of beer. This quick and easy recipe, using fresh ginger, does away with all that malarkey and makes a tasty ginger brew in two or three days. A word to the wise (and parents): this is, of course, mildly alcoholic. And please note all the cautions about exploding bottles.

1½ tbsp fresh ginger root, peeled and grated
7 oz (1 scant cup) granulated sugar
½ tsp cream of tartar
2 quarts cold water
1 lemon
½ tsp fast-action baker's yeast

1. Put the grated ginger, sugar, cream of tartar and 1 pint of the cold water in a large saucepan. Bring it to a boil.
2. Cut the lemon in half, squeeze the juice of both halves into the pan, then add in one-half to boil, discarding the other (the lemon flavor is too strong with both).
3. Simmer for 5–10 minutes, stirring to dissolve the sugar.
4. Add the remaining 1½ quarts of the cold water and let the liquid cool until it reaches room temperature.
5. Sprinkle on the yeast, stir it in, then leave the mixture for several hours covered well with a clean dishcloth.
6. Strain the liquid through a fine-mesh sieve or strainer, pressing down the ginger pieces in to extract any last bit of flavor.
7. Using a funnel or thin-lipped jug, pour into two 1-quart sterilized, plastic soft-drink bottles, leaving a little room at the top for the carbon dioxide to take up room. Make sure the last, yeasty-thick drops of the liquid are divided between the 2 bottles.
8. Seal and store in a cool, dark place for 2–3 days, loosening and resealing the tops from time to time to release the pressure of the gas. The ginger beer should be ready after 3 days.
9. Open with extreme caution at all times: the beer will be under pressure from the fermentation process, especially in hot weather. Never point a bottle at someone's face (including your own).

* *Never use glass bottles while ginger beer is fermenting, just in case they shatter. Once fermentation has died right down (after several days), you can decant to a prettier flip-top bottle if you like, but continue to treat with caution.*

* *Use your ginger beer as a mixer with spirits and with elderflower cordial, or simply add some bruised mint leaves and loads of ice.*

* *Cold ginger beer is incredibly refreshing on a hot day, and washes down mildly spicy seafood, such as stir-fried shrimp perfectly. Try it with quiches, too.*

* *You can also make a hedonistic ginger liqueur by mixing grated fresh ginger with vodka. Leave the mixture to steep for 5-6 days, strain into bottles and then, for each 1½ pints of vodka, add a solution made from 1 cup of water and ½ cup of sugar, shake and serve. Delicious!*

TEAS, TISANES AND SPICY BREWS

Boil water, pour it over a few fresh leaves or a sprinkling of aromatic spices, wait a few minutes, then drink. Making your own hot teas (or "tisanes," if you want to be fancy like Hercule Poirot) is about as easy as it gets. And the results are often a lot better than supermarket herbal teas. In my opinion, some of the latter are pretty unpleasant, and they can cost quite a bit, so why pay for a sullen yellow brew that smells like an old compost pile? It's much better to make your own fresh-tasting, aromatic version.

Some ingredients work better than others, of course. And certain teas have health benefits, or so it's claimed. Here, then, is a collection of the quickest, cheapest, simplest and tastiest "home brews," with some tips on how to serve them. Put the kettle on…

Mint Tea

Is mint tea the most refreshing drink in the world? Probably. It's versatile, too: a hot, minty brew really picks you up in cold weather, while frosty, iced mint tea is a thirst-quencher in the summer. The basic method hardly needs explaining—pour very hot water onto fresh mint leaves (about 5 leaves per cup)—but below are some tips that you might not have considered.

* *Always wash the mint and pick it over, removing any remotely woody stalks. Try to use the tender tips and first few leaves only, smaller stalks attached. For a stronger flavor, bruise the leaves a little with a spoon once they're in hot water.*
* *Try experimenting with different mint types. It's easy to find household mint, but Moroccan mint has a slightly better flavor. Or use spearmint.*
* *Use any combination of different mints and call it "Three Mint Tea" or "Four…" when you serve it to your friends. Sounds complex, but it's very easy.*
* *Make Iced Mint Tea: start with a hot brew, remove the mint leaves after a few minutes, then chill the tea. Put ice cubes into tumblers and pour in the cool tea, garnishing with fresh mint sprigs.*
* *Mint and lemon go well together, so try bruising a fresh lemon wedge with the back of a teaspoon as well as some mint sprigs in a cup of very hot water.*
* *A blend of black or green tea with fresh mint leaves is delicious.*
* *Sweeten any mint tea with sugar to taste. White sugar has a better flavor with mint than other sweetening agents.*

Lemon Verbena Tea

You'll need fresh leaves for lemon verbena tea; the dried stuff just doesn't cut it. This is a seasonal drink, and one that's treasured for its lovely aroma. The flavor is more delicate than the scent, with a distinctive citrus/lemon-peel tang. Use approximately 3 leaves per cup: no more, or the aroma gets a bit much. Tear each leaf into three or four pieces and put these in the cup or teapot before adding boiling water. Steep for a few minutes, then strain and serve. Most people prefer a spoonful of honey, too. Lemon verbena tea is said to help cure indigestion, insomnia, and bad nerves. I'll drink to that!

Raspberry-leaf Tea

There's plenty of anecdotal evidence to suggest that drinking raspberry-leaf tea can help bring on labor, and once contractions are underway, help soothe the pain; there's not much hard evidence for this, though. Whatever the case, the leaves of the raspberry plant (*Rubus idaeus*) are packed with vitamins and minerals, and in dried form they make a tasty, fruity tea. Please don't take it in earlier stages of pregnancy, just in case.

Pick the raspberry leaves and wash them. Leave them to dry out completely in a warm place, then scrunch them up. Add a couple of teaspoons of the crushed leaves to each mug of freshly boiled water, steep for a few minutes, then strain. Add honey to taste.

* *Kids seem to like this, too, and it's good for slightly upset tummies (anecdotal evidence again).*

Lemon Balm Tea

We have lots of lemon balm in the garden and often make tea from the fresh leaves. The delicate, citrus-based aroma and flavor are quite distinctive and make a gentle, soothing tea. Lemon balm tea is said to ward off just about everything from cold sores, menstrual cramps and insomnia to that scary catch-all "old age." Since the leaves come free and the flavor is very appealing, why not give it a try? I use approximately 8 leaves in a large teapot of freshly boiled water. You can serve this drink hot or iced. Add a slice of lemon and a sprig of mint in warm weather (lemon balm is a member of the mint family).

Chamomile Tea

Chamomile tea is said to be a relaxant and is also good for the digestive system, which explains why so many people have a cup late at night, especially after a big meal. This is one of the most popular packaged teas you can find, but a homemade version is so much better than bought dried chamomile products. Take a teaspoon or two of crushed leaves from a fresh chamomile plant and steep them in very hot water for 10 minutes. Cover while they're brewing to keep the volatile oils from dissipating. Add a little honey to taste, if desired. Note: anyone taking blood-thinning medication should not drink chamomile tea.

Fennel Tea

The slightly sweet, clean, aniseed flavor of tea made from crushed fennel seeds has real appeal. Use fennel seeds from plants you've grown for culinary use, hunt out wild fennel plants, or just use dried fennel seeds from the spice rack. Crush the seeds (one tablespoon per person) a little using a pestle and mortar, then put them in a mug and add freshly boiled water. Steep for 5 minutes, strain, then drink. This is said to help ease colic, gas, IBS and sore throats. Fennel is also believed to be an aphrodisiac (easing the gas undoubtedly helps here).

Try mixing fennel with ginger (a few slices of fresh or a teaspoon of ground), or even with a slice or two of the southwest Asian root galangal (or both) in a hot brew for a really warming cup.

Thyme and Sage Teas

The aromatic leaves of thyme make a tea that's especially good for colds, coughs and bronchial congestion. Use fresh or dried thyme and cover the teapot while it's steeping to retain the oils. Inhale the steam as you sip. Use lemon thyme with a squeeze of lemon juice for a freshly scented, tangier version.

Sage is the herb to go for if you have mouth ulcers or bad gums; I suggest both sipping and gargling with the brew. A more tasty blend is thyme and sage leaves (a few of each), with a lightly bruised rosemary sprig and 5 slices of fresh ginger to a normal-sized teapot. Steep for 8 minutes and pour.

Citrus and Spice Tea

This blend comes from the L'Epi Dupin restaurant in Paris. Take 1 slice each of fresh orange and lemon, 1 star anise, 1 sprig of fresh mint and approximately a third of a cinnamon stick of cinnamon. Stir everything into freshly boiled hot water, wait a few minutes and sip (you can strain it if you prefer).

Star Anise, Cinnamon and Ginger Tea

Place 1 star anise, approximately a third of a cinnamon stick, and 2 slices of peeled, fresh ginger root in a cup or mug. Add boiling water and let steep. Strain and sweeten with honey or (nice, this) a teaspoon of the syrup from a jar of preserved stem ginger.

Homemade Chai (simple version)

I like to make a pot of very weak black tea (so a little caffeine, yes), adding 2 fresh bay leaves, 2 cloves and 3 lightly crushed cardamom pods. Strain and add honey or sugar to taste. Easy.

Masala Chai

This tea is highly fragranced, sweet, and not too spicy if you go easy on the cloves (many recipes suggest far too much of this pungent spice). One very indulgent alternative is to replace the milk and sugar with half a cup of hot chocolate at the end. Either way, this makes two large mugfuls. It's especially good when you're snowed in and fed up, I've found.

½ cinnamon stick
6 whole cardamom pods
4 whole cloves
3 whole black peppercorns
2 cups water
1 cup milk
sugar to taste
3 tsp black tea

1. Lightly bruise the spices in a bowl with a large metal spoon.
2. Heat the water in a small saucepan, add the spices and bring to a gentle simmer for 8 minutes.
3. Add the milk and sugar to taste, stir, then bring to a simmer again briefly.
4. Add the black tea, stir, turn off the heat and let it all steep for a couple of minutes.
5. Strain, and serve with a cinnamon stick for stirring.

KITCHEN INFUSIONS

Take a simple bottle of spirit and transform it into a deeply aromatic liquid with a rich, golden hue, or even inky black, and with a myriad thrilling flavors. This elixir has versatile uses: it can be knocked back in a shot glass, mixed into cocktails, or gift-wrapped beautifully and given as a present. All this by simply raiding the kitchen cupboards and refrigerator for a few everyday ingredients.

Buy decent-quality base spirits for infusions at all times. This doesn't mean premium vodka or gin, by the way, but buy relatively inexpensive versions only from a reliable retailer with a high turnover, avoiding older bottles and bargain-basement "specials" (and the rough flavors that may ensue). Vodka is the perfect base for many infusions because it tastes and smells almost neutral, letting added ingredients shine through. Be aware that whiskey, gin and brandy will impart more of their own characters to any finished drink, for better or worse.

The following recipes are based on ingredients most of us have somewhere in the kitchen. Note: I've specified a standard European 70cl (1½ pint) bottle of spirit for each of these recipes, but you might have a little leftover each time. The important thing is to fill up your bottles or jars. Save the rest for the cook!

Black Pepper Vodka

Best enjoyed within
3 months

Wow, this turns black as night within days and makes a really hot, spicy spirit. Don't attempt to sip it on its own, even cautiously; you might reel back, sneezing. But this is useful stuff for splashing into a Bloody Mary, or for jazzing up a boring, healthy tomato or vegetable juice (see the tip on page 143 for making a Bloody Mary). Note: there's no sugar in this recipe. The aim is a very dry, intensely peppery liquid.

3½ oz black peppercorns
1½ pints vodka (unflavored)

1. Rifle through the peppercorns, removing any broken pieces and dust. You want whole corns.
2. Put the peppercorns into a large sterilized mason jar and fill it up with vodka.
3. Seal and shake gently to mix, then turn every day for 6 weeks to muddle up the peppercorns.
4. Strain off the peppercorns and discard. Bottle the black liquid.

* *For Bloody Mary mix: use this instead of other hot, spicy ingredients, but not with them! Make up the rest of the Bloody Mary, then add a dash of Black Pepper Vodka, taste and add a little more until you're happy with the balance.*
* *Chill in the refrigerator for a cooler mix with tomato/vegetable-based drinks.*
* *Use sparingly in rich gravies for roast beef, where it acts like a dab of horseradish, and you might put a shot into a spicy tomato chutney.*

Coffee Bean Vodka

Best enjoyed within
3 months

Coffee liqueurs are hugely popular and have a warming quality. Here's a delicious, easy, homemade version, which is not cloying, creamy or over-sweet. Instead, it tastes like rich mocha with intense chocolate and toffee qualities, but with a sense of freshly roasted beans, too.

60 coffee beans (I use good-quality, medium-strength Colombian)
1 heaped tsp sugar
1½ pints vodka (unflavored)

1. Tip the coffee beans into a large bowl and, using the back of a metal spoon, bash them until each one has cracked and broken a little.
2. Pour the cracked beans into a large sterilized mason jar and sprinkle with the sugar. Top up with the vodka until the jar is full.
3. Seal and shake gently. Store in a cool, dark place, turning daily for 4 days. Strain and bottle.

* *Add to hot, strong black coffee and pour whipped cream on top, sprinkling with a little cinnamon.*
* *This is a natural temptation with plain chocolate, ginger chocolate, chocolate coffee beans, chocolate-coated nuts, chilli chocolate. I could go on…*
* *Splash a little into rich meat stews (especially beef) for a Mexican hint of mocha that's barely discernible but nonetheless adds depth and power.*

Star Anise Vodka

Create a quick, perfumed, pastis-style spirit and use up any pretty leftover star anise for your next batch of Chinese cooking. The aniseed flavor is strong and \ natural, and very slightly sweet and spicy.

25 star anise
1½ pints vodka (unflavored)

1. Place the star anise in a large mason jar and pour in the vodka.
2. Seal, shake gently and leave for 3 days, turning twice a day.
3. Strain, bottle, and enjoy within 4 weeks.

* *This tastes slightly medicinal (but in a good way), and seems to soothe a sore throat.*

* *Chill this and add cold water to taste and some ice cubes for an instant French pastis/Greek ouzo experience.*

* *Save the discarded star anise for cooking. Add some to pork chops, or use in a Chinese-style marinade.*

Vanilla Rum

*Enjoy within
6 weeks of bottling.*

An autumnal golden color and slightly thickened texture make this tempting spirit infusion stand out. It's best enjoyed within a few weeks of making, since the truly lovely vanilla aroma fades with time. Note: no sugar again. This doesn't need sweetening.

4 vanilla pods
1½ pints white rum

1. Slice open the vanilla pods with the point of a small, sharp knife and scrape out all the tiny seeds. Retain everything and chop the pods into ¾-inch pieces.
2. Pour the rum into a large sterilized mason jar and add the chopped vanilla pods and the seeds.
3. Stir with a long spoon to loosen the sticky seeds, then seal and turn gently to start steeping.
4. Leave in a cool, dark place for 6 weeks, shaking the jar gently from time to time.
5. Strain through very fine muslin and bottle in attractive containers.

* *This is an great shot on its own, slightly cool, preferably with a box of fine milk and white chocolates.*
* *Serve with creamy cardamom panna cotta, Turkish delight, or ginger desserts.*

Spiced Rum

*Drink within
6 weeks of bottling.*

There are many commercial spiced rums on the shelves these days, but making your own is surprisingly quick and easy. Use golden rum instead of white; the richer, mellower flavor of the golden version counts for a lot here.

1½ pints golden rum
1 vanilla pod
2 cinnamon sticks, broken in half
1 whole star anise

2 cloves
1 allspice berry
** or 1 tbsp ground allspice**
2 large strips of rind from an orange

1. Pour the rum into a large sterilized jar and add all the remaining ingredients.
2. Seal, shake gently and leave for 48 hours to infuse.
3. The spiced rum is then ready and you can strain off the solid ingredients at this point using a fine muslin bag to remove as much of the ground all-spice powder as possible. Or leave the spices in for up to a week, but strain it at that point and bottle (see page 34).

* *Make a sweeter version by adding sugar to taste at the initial infusion stage. I prefer this drier, however.*
* *Use instead of golden rum in cocktails and drinks. It works well with ginger ale or tonic water, or as part of Long Island spiced tea!*

Cinnamon Schnapps

*Enjoy within
3 months*

You can use a clear, unflavored schnapps or unflavored vodka for this recipe, and even white rum works well. However, I think of this as less Caribbean and more Scandinavian. It's one of those shots that works well ice-cold on a freezing day. Standing in the snow, after singing Christmas carols, perhaps…

3 cinnamon sticks
1½ pints unflavored spirit

1. Break up the cinnamon sticks roughly, and pop them into a large sterilized jar.
2. Add the spirit and shake gently.
3. Steep for a week, turning the jar daily.
4. Strain off the cinnamon and bottle (see page 34).

* *Use the larger pieces of cinnamon in a mulled red wine, discarding any irritating tiny pieces.*
* *Bottle in clear glass, tie a cinnamon stick to the neck and give away as a gift.*
* *Mix with ginger beer for a spicy, peppery kick.*
* *Make into a hot toddy by dashing cinnamon schnapps into a china cup, then adding a slice of lemon, 1 clove and a little honey. Top up with very hot water, stir and inhale the steam before you sip.*

Cherry Brandy

*Drink within
6 months*

Christmas is the obvious time to drink (or cook with) cherry brandy, and beautifully wrapped bottles of a homemade version make particularly welcome presents. You could always give the brandy away while the cherries are still steeping in it, as they look so good, but do issue gentle instructions on when to remove the fruit.

¾ lb fresh, ripe red cherries   **1 tbsp caster sugar**
1 cinnamon stick   **1½ pints French brandy**

1. Wash the cherries and dry carefully. Remove any stalks and bruised fruit.
   Prick each cherry to help the juices start to flow.
2. Pack them into a sterilized mason jar and put the cinnamon stick on top.
3. Sprinkle the sugar over the fruit and top up to the brim with the brandy.
4. Seal and shake gently. Leave to steep for 6–8 weeks, turning the jar occasionally to mix.
5. Strain the fruit off after that time and bottle the brandy.

* *Savor on its own (at room temperature), with chocolate roulades and mousses, or British Christmas cake.*
* *Use the brandy-soaked cherries (after removing the stones) in fruitcakes, or chop up finely to add to mincemeat recipes.*
* *Add more sugar to the de-stoned cherries and reduce a little cherry brandy to make a sauce for pancakes.*
* *Splash into gravy to enjoy with steak; homemade gravy with cherry brandy is also good with pork.*

Cucumber Gin

*Drink within
6 weeks*

This is a big hit in our house. It's amazing how well cucumber shines through the relatively strong flavor and aroma of gin. Cucumber gin is so scented, summery, and refreshing— and it makes a great cocktail ingredient. Use very fresh, crisp cucumbers, and always, but always, remove every scrap of the green peel. Otherwise the result might be bitter.

3 small cucumbers
1½ pints gin (see below)

1. Peel the cucumbers and slice them lengthwise; take out the inner seed section of each. Cut into ¾-inch square pieces.
2. Put the cucumber pieces in a mason jar, add the gin, seal, and shake gently to mix.
3. Steep for a week in a very cool, dark place, turning occasionally, then strain off the cucumber and bottle the gin.

✳ *Don't feel like you have to use a premium gin for this, but try to get one with more than 40% alcohol: it will be an above-average spirit and have more character. If you want the very best, try Plymouth Gin or the already-rather-cucumbery Hendricks.*

✳ *You can drink this neat and very cold, especially in hot weather, but it is much better made into drinks:*

　* *Try one part cucumber gin to two parts tonic water with a sprig of bruised mint and plenty of ice.*

　* *Even better, one part cucumber gin, one part concentrated homemade Elderflower Cordial (see page 43) and two parts tonic, with mint and ice: a divine, cooling concoction, especially in high summer.*

　* *For a sweeter version of these cocktails, use lemonade instead of tonic water.*

　* *Cucumber gin is also great topped up with dry ginger ale. Chill both ingredients.*

FESTIVE DRINKS FOR ENTERTAINING

A true festive drink is one for enjoying at precious moments when you're in a crowd, whether you are celebrating Christmas, treating a group of dinner guests at the end of a big feast, or kicking off a party in style. Boring, bought, big-brand wines just don't cut it on a special occasion—so make something instead to show how much the moment means.

It was quite difficult to choose which drinks to put in this chapter. We all have a different moment we consider to be the most festive, so I've included something for everyone (I hope!). There's a clever spiced syrup concentrate for that ever-popular winter warmer, Mulled Wine; Eggnog for the same season, but to satisfy those who adore passing around a creamy, rich liqueur; homemade Amaretto for those wonderful (and otherwise expensive) after-dinner digestifs; and a new take on a key ingredient for original Bloody Mary. Oh, and a soft, fizzy, but surprisingly healthy homemade "soda" for kids' celebrations. Let's party!

Mulled Wine and Mulling Syrup

Makes 2 cups

*Keeps for
2–3 months
in a dark
store cupboard*

Hot, spicy, aromatic mulled wine is a real holiday treat. But watch out: commercial mulled red wines or kits for making them often turn out horribly sweet or overladen with oily clove. Tea-bag-style sachets don't quite cut it, either, with one or two exceptions. Anyway, it's more fun to make your own concentrated base for hot, spicy, mulled drinks. This recipe is adapted from one by Lulu Grimes; it makes the house smell wonderfully Christmassy while it's being concocted.

Simply reheat the quantity of mulling syrup shown below with a normal-sized bottle of decent red wine or hard cider, adding a few fresh citrus-fruit slices to the pan. And don't forget to boast loudly that you made it all yourself!

**9 oz (1 heaped cup) superfine sugar
2 ripe, juicy oranges, cut into quarters
6 whole cloves
6 allspice berries or 1 tbsp ground allspice
2 cinnamon sticks, broken in half
2 tsp freshly ground nutmeg
2-inch piece of fresh ginger root, peeled and sliced
1 pint cold water**

1. Put all the ingredients into a large pan and bring to just below boiling, stirring well to dissolve the sugar.
2. Simmer gently to reduce by half. Stir from time to time.
3. Leave to cool, then strain through very fine muslin twice before bottling.

* *Don't worry about the finished syrup being slightly cloudy; this is normal and won't show up once your red wine or cider and fruit are added.*
* *Use medium-bodied, ripe, hugely fruity red wine for mulling (and a fresh bottle, please).*
* *Add a good slug of brandy or port for an extra kick.*
* *When making the final mull, never let it boil. The alcohol will dissipate and it might taste slightly burned and jammy.*
* *Serve the finished mull in thick, heatproof glass tumblers, and give guests a cinnamon stick for stirring.*
* *Try a white wine mull using a fairly rich, juicy white such as Chardonnay, Viognier, or South African Chenin Blanc as the base. Add a couple of star anise and two-thirds the quantity of mulling syrup (above) to a normal-sized bottle of white wine, with honey to taste. Heat very gently.*
* *A "mock mull" is a great soft version. Heat up homemade Blackberry or Blackcurrant Cordial (see page 66), diluted to taste, or Red Grape Juice (see page 106), or buy some if you're stuck). Add star anise, cinnamon, honey, and cloves, tasting as you add the spices until you get the right balance. This goes for any mull: if in doubt, introduce the other ingredients to the liquid slowly, and taste regularly until the right flavor is achieved.*
* *Also try other mulled recipes: Hard Apple Cider on page 94 and Mead on page 112.*

Eggnog

NB: this recipe
contains raw egg

Makes approx
1 quart

Keep in the
refrigerator until the
fresh ingredients'
sell-by date

Given the current UK craze for keeping chickens, I know quite a few people with a ludicrous oversupply of eggs who can't give them away to their equally eggs-cessive neighbors. Don't make yet another omelette; try a homemade Eggnog instead. Beware: this is very sweet (all that sugar!), strong (rum and brandy!) and rich (oceans of cream!). It's decadent, but oh-so-good. This makes enough for a small crowd.

6 fresh, free-range eggs
7 oz (1 scant cup) superfine sugar
1 tsp freshly grated nutmeg, plus more to garnish
½ tsp vanilla extract
½ pint heavy cream
1¾ cups whole milk
½ cup dark rum
½ cup brandy

1. Beat the eggs well in a large bowl until frothy. Add the sugar and beat again, then add the nutmeg and vanilla and mix well.
2. Now beat in the cream, followed by the milk and finally, trickle in the rum and brandy, bit by bit, mixing all the time.
3. Store in the refrigerator for a couple of hours to chill. Pour into glasses and grate a little nutmeg on top before handing glasses around.

* *Pour the cream and milk, and then the rum and brandy, slowly and gradually to avoid the possibility of curdling.*
* *Serve in small amounts since this is so rich—a little glassful per guest does just fine.*

Cumin Lassi

Makes just over 1 pint

Always keep Lassi in the refrigerator and use within 2 hours of making

Now for a healthy, cooling drink or two that works well when friends or family visit and want an alcohol-free but impressive option. A yogurt-based, cooling lassi is a traditional drink of India's Punjab, one that manages to create something addictive and deeply refreshing out of the most unpromising ingredients. A lassi can be alluring, especially in hot, humid weather, or as a drink with a light, healthy lunch. I've been through diverse recipes, including versions made with thick, rich yogurt and even cream, but this cumin lassi and the variations that follow it (two salty, one sweet) are my favorites. I make no claims for the authenticity of these recipes, but they do taste good!

1 heaped tsp cumin seeds
½ pint plain, low-fat yogurt
½ pint 2% milk
2 tsp lemon juice
large pinch of fine salt
1 small teacup of ice cubes
fresh mint sprigs (optional garnish)

1. Roast the cumin seeds in a dry frying pan for a few minutes, until they're just turning brown and giving off a rich aroma.
2. Pour them into a mortar and crush them up with a pestle.
3. Put in a blender with all the other ingredients, including the ice cubes, and whizz.
4. Pour into tall, cold tumblers. Garnish with fresh mint.

* *This works well when entertaining: it's quick and easy to whip up.*
* *To make a saffron lassi, use the recipe above but with half the cumin. Soak 15 saffron strands in about 1½ pints of warm milk. Leave to soak for 1-2 hours. Add this to the blender with the other ingredients.*
* *For a mint lassi, use the recipe above, but substitute 2 tbsp fresh, finely chopped mint leaves for the cumin.*

Mango Lassi

Makes 1 pint

Always keep lassi in the refrigerator and use within 2 hours of making

A delicious, refreshing treat. Young and old love it, so make it when your family turns up.

½ pint plain, low-fat yogurt
1 cup fresh, ripe mango pieces
1 small teacup of crushed ice
2 tbsp superfine sugar

1. Chop the mango pieces very finely, retaining the juice that comes out.
2. Put all the ingredients in a blender and whizz until smooth.
3. Pour into chilled tall glass tumblers.

* *Make sure the mango you use is ripe; buy it in advance and ripen it at home, then leave it out in a warm room before cutting it up. Underripe fruit will ruin the drink.*

Amaretto

*Always shake
before serving*

*Makes just
over 1 pint*

*Keeps well
for 3 months*

Not only is the almond-rich, fragrant amaretto liqueur a popular digestif, but it is also a versatile cooking ingredient and great in cocktails, too. So, here's an easy recipe for homemade amaretto. The real thing is created with oil of apricot kernels or almonds, or both; I use a natural almond extract instead. Make sure this (and the vanilla extract) are top-quality: no fakes! You'll be surprised at how impressive this drink is for the minimal effort it requires.

1 cup water
7 oz (1 scant cup) sugar
3½ oz (½ cup) light brown sugar
1¾ cups vodka (unflavored)
¼ cup (2 fl oz) almond extract
2 tsp vanilla extract

1. Bring the water to a boil in a saucepan and add both the sugars. Take off the heat and stir well until the sugar has all dissolved. Leave to cool.
2. Add the vodka and stir. Add the two extracts and stir well.
3. Pour the amaretto into a jug, then through a funnel into a bottle and seal. The mix is ready to use immediately.

✱ *The extracts will eventually separate whatever you do, so always shake or mix well before using.*

✱ *Try a splash in creamy chocolate desserts, or poach peaches in a syrup containing a tablespoonful or two.*

✱ *A sip of this is divine at the end of dinner, served with little crunchy amaretti biscuits.*

Cherryade

Makes 1½ pints,
before diluting

Best enjoyed as
soon as it is made

A versatile drink. On its own, it's a tangy, pink drink for adults and kids, and best served outdoors in the garden or on a picnic. But you can also dash in spirit to make it into a delectable, alcoholic summer cocktail. Cherries have a unique, fragrant appeal, and this drink is lightly perfumed and deeply refreshing. Do I really need to say that it's way better than the fiercely fizzy, artificially flavored sodas?

½ lb fresh, ripe cherries
2½ cups boiling water
1 lime
2 oz (¼ cup) superfine sugar
sparkling water, to dilute

1. Wash the cherries carefully and remove all stalks. Chop each one in half and remove the stones. Put the fruit in a big bowl and bruise them slightly with the back of a metal spoon to get the juices flowing.
2. Pour the hot water over the cherries and stir.
3. Peel the lime and quarter it. Add a couple of strips of peel and the juice of one quarter to the cherries.
4. Add the sugar and stir until it has dissolved. Cover and leave for 2 hours.
5. Strain. Add cold sparkling water to dilute to your own taste.

* *Tradition says to use a tarragon sprig in this recipe; it adds a light aniseed note. If you want to try this, squash the tarragon leaves gently and add them at stage 3.*
* *If you're heading away from home for a picnic, pack the cherry base and the cold sparkling water separately and mix up the drink once you're found the perfect spot.*
* *For a Cherry Cocktail, add a splash of good Cognac to each glass of the cherry base before topping up with just a little sparkling water. Garnish with a twist of lime peel.*
* *You can use an orange or mandarin orange instead of lime here, but the sharp bite of lemon tastes wrong.*
* *This works pretty well with cherries that have been canned in fruit juice, too; use the pitted cherries from a 1-lb can, and approximately 4 tablespoons of the juice inside. However, fresh cherries are much better.*

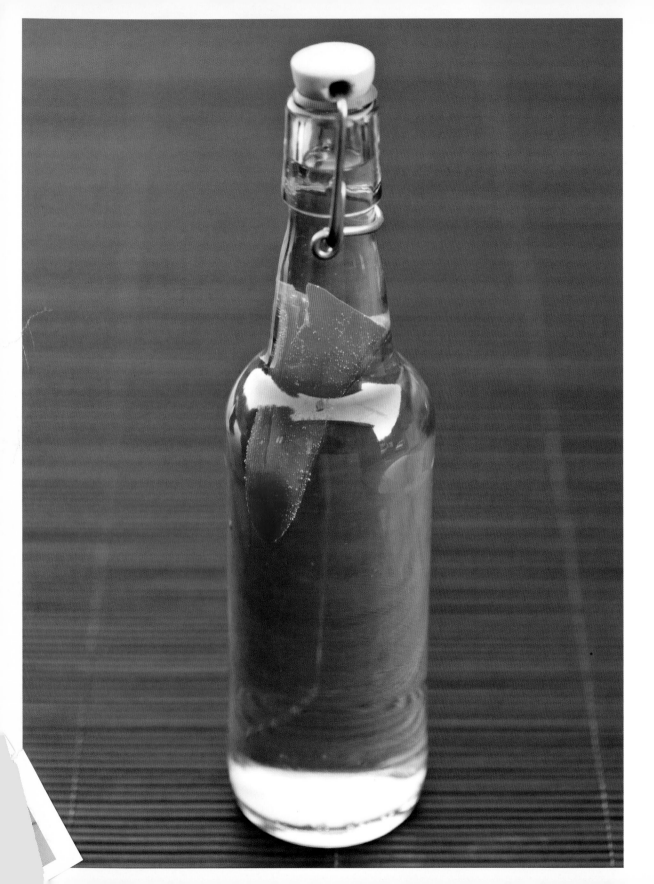

Red Chili Sherry

Store in the refrigerator, for up to 4 weeks

This was recommended to me by Angus McCaig, who runs The Holt gastro-pub in Honiton, Devon, England. The Holt specializes in smoked food of every variety, and Angus uses smoked chili peppers for his sherry infusion – a fabulous drink with depth and intensity. However, fresh chilies are also great used in this infusion, and the result is the perfect ingredient for a Bloody Mary. I make it in small quantities because it doesn't last well, and only a little is needed at a time.

1 small, medium-hot red chili pepper, approximately 2½-inches long
1¾ cups pale, dry sherry (fino or manzanilla)

1. Wash and dry the chili pepper; cut off the stalk.
2. Slice into the sides a couple of times (do not remove seeds).
3. Pour out a little of the sherry into a clean jug to make room for the chili.
4. Push the chili down the neck of the bottle and into the sherry.
   If it won't fit, cut it lengthwise.
5. Top up with the sherry from the jug and reseal with the original cork stopper.
6. Shake gently, and leave to steep for 2–3 weeks, turning occasionally or whenever the mood takes you.
7. Pour some sherry out (retaining it, of course!) and remove the chili using a metal kebab stick. Discard. Top up and seal.

* *Cheaper dry sherry, as long as it's freshly opened and youthful, is fine for this; there's no point in shelling out on a fine label.*

* *The chili looks fabulous while in the bottle, so display the steeping infusion!*

* *This also adds a great kick to gazpacho or cold tomato soup. Go easy on it, though: it's strong.*

* *Red chili sherry isn't that nice on its own, unless you crave a very spicy shot. But add it to a Bloody Mary or other tomato/vegetable juice base and it's great. Add dash by dash, as you would with bitters to a cocktail mix, tasting until it's just right. It's important (nay, crucial) in life to know how to make a superlative Bloody Mary, so here goes:*

  > *Fill tall tumblers with ice.*
  > *Pour a large shot of good unflavored vodka into each one.*
  > *Mix up a jug of tomato juice with a good twist of white pepper, a large pinch of celery salt, the juice of half a lime and a splash of your homemade Red Chili Sherry (see above).*
  > *Stir, taste, adjust seasoning and add more lime juice and/or fino if needed.*
  > *If you like a huge spicy kick, dash in a few drops of Tabasco. Stir again.*
  > *Pour this mix into the tumblers, over the vodka.*
  > *Hand around the glasses with small sticks of celery as stirrers.*

  > *I've tried making my own tomato juice, but the bought stuff is excellent and cheap anyway. Concentrate on making the Red Chili Sherry instead.*

ENJOYING YOUR DRINKS

SERVING

No one with any sense would uncork Champagne that was warm, or offer a ripe red Burgundy from a shot glass. Homemade drinks need serving the right way, too, which doesn't mean that you need to make a great fuss about them. Just follow a few simple rules of thumb and you'll get the best out of each one.

STAY COOL

Almost all the drinks in this book taste much better when they are served properly chilled. Chilling a drink emphasizes its refreshing, mouth-watering acidity. This goes for the fermented Fruit Wines, Citrus Cordials, Orchard Drinks, Grape Drinks, Lassis and Floral Drinks (except Rose Teas). The Infusions are a matter of personal taste: I prefer my Cucumber Gin very cold, but I like Damson Gin at room temperature, for example. To make a mixed drink taste even colder, chill the mixers and even the glasses.

CLOSING TIME

Don't open any homemade drinks before you need to: there are no heavy, tannic wines in this book, or, for that matter, anything that benefits from "breathing." Homemade drinks tend to be more delicate than bought wines, so minimize oxidation (the deteriorative effects of oxygen on wine). Open and serve your drinks only at the last possible minute.

DRINKING TIME

If you're serving drinks that have been opened on previous occasions, check them for freshness. Homemade wines, ciders and juices can be fairly fragile, and without artificial preservatives or sulphur, they clearly don't keep well after opening. All in all, don't expect opened bottles to taste great three weeks after your last party!

READY, SET, POUR

Have all your accessories ready in advance of pouring. That means not only cleaned and polished glasses but trays, stirrers, fruit and knives for chopping and other garnishes. More on these items follows, but the most basic rule of serving well is to be prepared.

Glasses

It's the same for almost all fine drinks, homemade or otherwise: the best glasses for the job are, er, *glass* (not plastic or laminated paper); thin, because this feels nicer on the lips than thick glass; long-stemmed, so you can hold the glass without warming the liquid and easily see the glints of color and light in it; and plain, because cut-glass or colored glass obscures your view of the drink's appearance.

Simple, good-quality, tall wine glasses are perfect for all the homemade wines and cordials in this book, and they also appeal for serving grown-up soft drinks, ciders and perries, too.

You might prefer beer mugs for Nettle Beer, Orchard Drinks such as Cider, and even Mead; if so, clear, plain glass is still the way to go. Thicker, chunkier, heatproof glass tumblers are needed for hot drinks, though, and these can also look good for spirit infusions served "on the rocks." Use tall highball tumblers (ideally plain glass again) for mixed drinks, and don't shy away from proper Champagne flutes for sparklers such as elderflower bubbly or those diluted with sparkling water or soda. Tall, slim flutes are better than wide, flatter coupes, because bubbles don't disappear in a blink.

Okay, okay: for small children, or by the pool, or on a picnic, clear plastic glasses are by far the best option for those moments when glass really isn't suitable. In general, they're much better than paper cups.

Chill the glasses themselves for very cold drinks: the frosty effect looks great. Simply place them in the refrigerator for a good hour before using.

A final word about washing dishes: don't use too much detergent! Soapy residue on glasses can ruin the flavor and scent of a delicate homemade drink, and it will kill any bubbles. Very clean glasses are important, of course, but a tiny amount of dishwashing liquid and lots of hot water can go a long way. Always use clean linen dishcloths for drying, and check that all traces of lipstick are gone at this stage.

Accessories

Maraschino cherries, paper umbrellas, silver sparklers…put them right out of your mind (unless you're planning a 1980s' revival night). Accessories for modern homemade drinks are low-key, subtle, simple, and preferably all-natural. You might need all the help you can get convincing skeptics about the joys of elderflower cordial, mead, or oak leaf wine, so try some of the ideas opposite to liven up your concoctions.

Tastings

If organizing a "professional" tasting of homemade drinks, you'll need spittoons for those who don't want to swallow all the samples. Clean jugs or even glass vases or little buckets are fine if you don't own real spittoons, and you might want to put paper towels into the bottom of each container. If it's a serious tasting or competition, stock up on notebooks and pens.

Gatherings

Find time to enjoy your homemade results in relaxed settings. When there's a crowd coming, encourage everyone to help themselves. Set up a "bar," with glasses, chilled mixers, fruit garnishes, mint—everything anyone could need. Show off your finest concoctions, then tell your guests to help themselves so that you can have a good time, too. Keep all drinks cool by setting some bottles outside in cold weather, or filling large buckets with ice and pushing bottles in them.

Celebrations

Move back into center stage for any toasts or special announcements. This is the time to crack open fresh bottles, sparkling or otherwise, and even bring out a clean set of glasses on a tray. Try (just ahead of the big moment) mixing your homemade drinks for this: a dash of damson or sloe gin in Champagne flutes topped up with dry cava, for example, or elderflower spritzers for non-drinkers.

ICE CUBES
Make them more interesting by using concentrated cordial, or freeze water with tiny, perfect berries inside (redcurrants, baby gooseberries or raspberries, for example).

FLOATS
Sprigs of little flowers such as elderflower or individual rose petals on drinks, as well as mint sprigs, all make attractive garnishes.

GARNISHES
Fresh citrus-fruit or apple slices are the easiest. Also try twists of peel pared away from unwaxed organic limes, lemons, tangerines or oranges. Little bunches of baby redcurrants, or tiny individual berries bobbing about in sparkling drinks look good, too. Balance a kiwi-fruit slice on the side of a glass, or slash the bottom of a strawberry and stick that on.

SALT OR SUGAR RIM
Try this on your cocktail glasses or tumblers for extra pizzazz! Pour some coarse-grained salt or superfine sugar into a saucer, rub a slice of lemon or lime around the outside rim of the glass and turn it upside down to dip firmly in the saucer. Salt works best with refreshing tangy, dry drinks such as elderflower-based cocktails or rhubarb wine. Use sugar with sweeter drinks such as strawberry wine.

STIRRERS
Simple but neat and natural stirrers for homemade drinks include small, celery sticks for a Bloody Mary, and cinnamon sticks for hot toddies. Use your imagination, or invest in some attractive long-handled teaspoons, especially if you plan to try "muddling" (bruising) mint leaves or wedges of citrus fruit.

SPRING AND SUMMER ENTERTAINING

It's vital to keep drinks tasting fresh and cool when it's hot outside and guests are thirsty. Chill everything-drinks, mixers, glasses-twice as hard as usual, and only pull each item out of the refrigerator at the last minute. Keep bottles in the shade, or in proper or improvised ice buckets.

KEEPING IT LIGHT

The right drinks for summer parties and picnics are the lighter, more gently aromatic, elegant styles, preferably with a good crisp streak of acidity to emphasize the refreshing quality in your wine, cordial, or mixed drink.
Think dry and medium-dry, light white and pink homemade wines, ciders, perries, and of course, cordials, plus cold lavender and cucumber infusions for drinks with a clean, mouth-watering finish.

SOFT DRINKS

Never forget to provide these as well as alcoholic drinks for guests in warm weather. And for the drinkers, dilute strong alcoholic drinks with loads of chilled sparkling water, lemonade or soda to counteract the heat. No one wants dehydration and an instant headache in the middle of the day.
Iced Mint Tea or Masala Chai (see pages 118-121) are great ideas, too.

ON A PICNIC

Take homemade concentrates and mixers separately and mix them together when you're settled. Put the resealed bottles in a stream or pool to keep them cool and always cover up any sweet and aromatic drinks once opened to keep the ants and flies away!

FOOD

Delectable summer party snacks to enjoy with the homemade drinks from this book should be elegant and light. Avoid very sweet or rich, spicy dishes.
Try light, savory canapes, cold shrimp and smoked fish, delicate little savory pastries, sushi and fresh fruit.

FALL AND WINTER ENTERTAINING

When it's cold outside, think hot toddies or soothing or spicy drinks such as those made from ginger, or based on strong, wintry spirits such as whiskey and rum. Think creamy Eggnog or sweet and spicy amaretto. Homemade drinks should be heavily perfumed, rich, and heartwarming. The best homemade wines for colder weather months are elderberry, blackberry and plum.

INDULGE

Stock up on miniature marshmallows, ground cinnamon and cloves for sweet, creamy and hot winter drinks. Grate chocolate and nutmeg on your drinks and stir them with cinnamon or peppermint sticks.

MULLS AND HOT TODDIES

Never boil these drinks too much or the alcohol will steam off and disappear into the night...

NON-ALCOHOLIC

Don't forget to provide good winter drinks for children and teetotallers, such as Fruity Ginger Ale, or Cherryade, or Blackberry Cordial, or Pink Grapefruit and Pomegranate Cordial. Anything that looks darker, richer, and pinker can warm up the winter chill.

FOOD

Great cold-weather party snacks to munch with these homemade drinks include mildly spiced vegetable samosas, Chili shrimp, olives with plenty of garlic, salted nuts, smoked or cured meats, and dried or preserved fruits. And with any sweet and (or) creamy drinks: chocolate, of course!

MATCHING DRINKS WITH FOOD

We're all fairly used to matching "normal" bought table wines to food these days, but what about homemade drinks? Some of them work just as well at the dining table, and make terrific partners for certain dishes or types of cuisine. Here are some suggestions on where to start.

MEAT

	Page
Blackcurrant Cordial	54
Crème de Cassis	62
All blackberry drinks	66–9
Elderberry Wine	70
Red Grape Juice	106

CHICKEN, TURKEY AND DUCK

Plum Wine	58
Oak Leaf Wine	75
All Orchard drinks	90-101
Parsnip Wine	104

FISH, SEAFOOD, VEGETABLE AND SALADS

All elderflower drinks	43–5
Dandelion Wine	46
Gooseberry Wine	57
Plum Wine	58
Rhubarb Wine	60
All citrus cordials	83–7
Fruity Ginger Ale	113
Ginger Beer	114

SPICY FOOD

Plum Wine	58
Mandarin Orange and Lime Cordial	84
Lime, Ginger and Lemongrass Cordial	86
Rice and Raisin Wine	108
Fruity Ginger Ale	113
Ginger Beer	114
Cumin Lassi	137

CHEESES

	Page
All elderflower drinks (mild cheeses and goats cheeses)	43–5
Dandelion Wine (mild cheeses and goats cheeses)	46
Plum Wine	58
Elderberry Wine	70
Nettle Beer	74
Oak Leaf Wine (smoked cheese)	75
Damson Gin	77
All Orchard Drinks	90–101
Mead	112

DESSERTS

Lavender Lemonade	50
Strawberry Wine (drink with fresh fruit)	56
Crème de Cassis	62
Crème de Mure	68
Rosehip Syrup	72
Damson Gin	77
Quince Vodka	78
Limoncello	88
Amaretto	138

MATCHING DRINKS TO THE OCCASION

Of course it's your choice, but here are my suggestions for drinks that work especially well on certain occasions.

FURTHER READING

Every wannabe winemaker should try to get hold of the classic *First Steps in Winemaking* by C.J.J. Berry (Special Interest Model Books, new ed 2002). This is a great beginner's guide that has converted two or three generations to the cause!

Other useful references:

Wilson, C. *Favourite Country Wines and Cordials.* J. Salmon Ltd, 2001

Garey, T. *The Joy of Home Winemaking.* Avon Books, 1996

Pooley, M. & Lomax, J. *Real Cider Making on a Small Scale.* Special Interest Model Books, 1999

Beauviale, A. *Mes Boissons Maison.* Christine Bonneton, 2007

Diffords, S. *Cocktails.* Sauce Guides, 9th ed 2010

Atkins, S. *Cocktails & Perfect Party Drinks.* Quadrille, 2005

I also raided a selection of very old drink-making books dating from the 1960s–80s and would like to thank those friends, neighbors and relations who loaned some of these.

INDEX

ACKNOWLEDGMENTS

Huge thanks to the whole team at Mitchell Beazley for all their input and energy, and to Noel Murphy for his truly lovely photography. I also raise my glass to the many kind neighbors who helped me with advice and/or produce, but particular mention goes to smallholder extraordinaire Sam Robson, and my local assistant on this book, Julie Cooney, aka the queen of strawberry wine! Thanks, too, to Nick Borst-Smith and to Ian Kendall of Homebrew in Exeter. Finally, a toast to my country-loving, produce-growing, wild-foraging parents, Brian and Pat, who, sometime around 1975, persuaded a sulky 10-year-old to help make dandelion wine…